S0-BSD-910

THE LAW OF SPECIAL EDUCATION

2nd Edition

by
Margaret C. Jasper

Oceana's Legal Almanac Series:
Law for the Layperson

2004
Oceana Publications, Inc.
Dobbs Ferry, New York

Information contained in this work has been obtained by Oceana Publications from sources believed to be reliable. However, neither the Publisher nor its authors guarantee the accuracy or completeness of any information published herein, and neither Oceana nor its authors shall be responsible for any errors, omissions or damages arising from the use of this information. This work is published with the understanding that Oceana and its authors are supplying information, but are not attempting to render legal or other professional services. If such services are required, the assistance of an appropriate professional should be sought.

Library of Congress Control Number: 2004105892

ISBN 978-0-379-11386-0

Oceana's Legal Almanac Series: Law for the Layperson

ISSN 1075-7376

©2004 by Oceana Publications, Inc.

To My Husband Chris

Your love and support
are my motivation and inspiration

-and-

In memory of my son, Jimmy

Table of Contents

CHAPTER 5:

THE FAMILY EDUCATIONAL RIGHTS AND PRIVACY ACT OF 1974

CHAPTER 6:

TYPES OF DISABILITIES

CHAPTER 7:
EDUCATING THE SPECIAL NEEDS CHILD

APPENDICES

ABOUT THE AUTHOR

MARGARET C. JASPER is an attorney engaged in the general practice of law in South Salem, New York, concentrating in the areas of personal injury and entertainment law. Ms. Jasper holds a Juris Doctor degree from Pace University School of Law, White Plains, New York, is a member of the New York and Connecticut bars, and is certified to practice before the United States District Courts for the Southern and Eastern Districts of New York, the United States Court of Appeals for the Second Circuit, and the United States Supreme Court.

Ms. Jasper has been appointed to the panel of arbitrators of the American Arbitration Association and the law guardian panel for the Family Court of the State of New York, is a member of the Association of Trial Lawyers of America, and is a New York State licensed real estate broker and member of the Westchester County Board of Realtors, operating as Jasper Real Estate, in South Salem, New York. She maintains a website at http://www.JasperLawOffice.com.

Ms. Jasper is the author and general editor of the following legal almanacs: AIDS Law; The Americans with Disabilities Act; Animal Rights Law; The Law of Attachment and Garnishment; Bankruptcy Law for the Individual Debtor; Individual Bankruptcy and Restructuring; Banks and their Customers; Buying and Selling Your Home; The Law of Buying and Selling; The Law of Capital Punishment; The Law of Child Custody; Commercial Law; Consumer Rights Law; The Law of Contracts; Copyright Law; Credit Cards and the Law; The Law of Debt Collection; Dictionary of Selected Legal Terms; The Law of Dispute Resolution; The Law of Drunk Driving; DWI, DUI and the Law; Education Law; Elder Law; Employee Rights in the Workplace; Employment Discrimination Under Title VII; Environmental Law; Estate Planning; Everyday Legal Forms; Executors and Personal Representatives: Rights and Responsibilities; Harassment in the Workplace; Health Care and Your Rights. Home Mortgage Law Primer; Hospital Liability

Law; Identity Theft and How To Protect Yourself; Insurance Law; The Law of Immigration; International Adoption; Juvenile Justice and Children's Law; Labor Law; Landlord-Tenant Law; The Law of Libel and Slander; Living Together: Practical Legal Issues; Marriage and Divorce; The Law of Medical Malpractice; Motor Vehicle Law; The Law of No-Fault Insurance; Nursing Home Negligence; The Law of Obscenity and Pornography; Patent Law; The Law of Personal Injury; Privacy and the Internet: Your Rights and Expectations Under the Law; Probate Law; The Law of Product Liability; Real Estate Law for the Homeowner and Broker; Religion and the Law; The Right to Die; Law for the Small Business Owner; Social Security Law; Special Education Law; The Law of Speech and the First Amendment; Teenagers and Substance Abuse; Trademark Law; Victim's Rights Law; The Law of Violence Against Women; Welfare: Your Rights and the Law; What if it Happened to You: Violent Crimes and Victims' Rights; What if the Product Doesn't Work: Warranties & Guarantees; Workers' Compensation Law; and Your Child's Legal Rights: An Overview.

INTRODUCTION

More than five million children receive special education services. Approximately 2.5 million of these children have learning disabilities. Others suffer speech and language disabilities; autism; attention deficit disorder (ADD), hearing and visual impairments, emotional disturbance and mental retardation. This almanac seeks to clarify the legal rights and responsibilities set forth in special education laws, which must be understood in order for one to effectively advocate for these children.

This almanac sets forth a brief history of the emergence of special education, and the development of legislation governing the education of disabled students. Through legislation and litigation, the rights of disabled children to a free, appropriate education have expanded considerably. Parents have been afforded certain rights in connection with their child's educational process, including access to records, assessment procedures, independent evaluation, notice and consent requirements, due process hearings, and placement rights.

This almanac examines landmark special education legislation, such as the Individuals with Disabilities Education Act (IDEA). The IDEA is the primary piece of legislation governing special education in the nation's schools. The IDEA confers the right to a free appropriate public education to each child, and sets forth a procedure—the Individualized Education Program ("IEP")—whereby a child's educational progress is evaluated and closely monitored and updated.

In addition, provisions for the protection of disabled children under Section 504 of the Rehabilitation Act are also discussed. All children with disabilities are protected under Section 504 whether or not they are covered under the IDEA. This almanac also discusses the impact of "No Child Left Behind Act," which recently reauthorized the Elementary and Secondary Education Act (ESEA), upon the education of disabled and disadvantaged children.

The confidentiality of school records under the Family Educational Records Privacy Act (FERPA)—including a disabled student's IEP—is also set forth in this almanac. In brief, under FERPA, schools must honor parental requests to inspect and review their child's educational records within strict time limitations.

This almanac also explores the role of the United States Department of Education, and its various departments, in protecting the rights of disabled children.

The Appendix provides resource directories, applicable statutes, and other pertinent information and data. The Glossary contains definitions of many of the terms used throughout the almanac.

CHAPTER 1:
OVERVIEW

EDUCATION LAW

Education law is derived from both federal and state sources. The United States Constitution is the governing law of the land, and many aspects of our current education law have evolved from its tenets. In addition, Congress has enacted a number of laws which deal with education. These laws are published in the United States Code by Title number. Education Law is published under Title 20 of the U.S. Code.

States must develop education statutes that are consistent with the United States Code (U.S.C.). State statutes may provide more rights than the corresponding federal law, but states may not give lesser rights than those provided for by federal law.

Regulations are enacted to clarify and explain statutes. Although regulations may give force and effect to a statute, they must also be consistent with the statute. Federal Regulations are published in the Code of Federal Regulations (CFR).

For example, Title 20 of the U. S. Code requires the U. S. Department of Education to develop and publish special education regulations giving force and effect to the Individuals with Disabilities Education Act (the "IDEA"). States must also develop special education regulations that are consistent with the Code of Federal Regulations.

COMPULSORY EDUCATION LAWS

Historically, poor children did not attend school regularly, and often dropped out before graduation. In an effort to make sure all children attended school, state legislatures passed compulsory attendance laws. Under these laws, parents were obligated to send their children to school or face prosecution. Presently, all children who fall between a state's age range for compulsory education are required to attend school on a regular basis. Children generally begin their formal education at age 6. In most states, the maximum age a child is required to attend school is 16.

A table setting forth the compulsory education age range, by state, is set forth at Appendix 1.

Disabled children, however, were often either absent from school or not enrolled at all. Disabled children who did attend school were generally put into special education classes with other disabled children, regardless of the nature or extent of their disabilities. Disabled children were never placed in classes with non-disabled children.

Despite the compulsory attendance laws, most states allowed school authorities to exclude children if they believed that the child would not benefit from education, or if the child's presence would disrupt the non-disabled children or interfere with teaching. In fact, in some states, it was actually illegal for a parent to enroll a disabled child in public school once that child had been excluded.

In an effort to make sure all disabled children are afforded an education, state legislatures passed compulsory special education laws under which schools are obligated to provide special education services to all children. Presently, all children who fall between a state's age range for compulsory special education services are entitled to receive a free, appropriate education. Generally, the ages for compulsory special education services begins early, e.g., from birth to 3 years old in some states, and ends later, e.g. 21 years old in most states.

A table setting forth the compulsory special education services age range, by state, is set forth at Appendix 2.

VOCATIONAL SCHOOLS

The predecessor to present-day special education programs was the "vocational" school. Vocational schools were more likely to be found in the urban environment. The students were generally children from depressed areas who were perceived as unable to function in a purely academic program. Often, such children were labeled as "learning disabled."

These children were generally not steered towards college and, in many cases, actually discouraged from pursuing higher education, because college was not seen as a likely prospect for their future. The vocational training was designed to prevent delinquency and give these underprivileged children the necessary training to enable them to enter the skilled labor workforce upon graduation from high school.

CASE LAW AND LEGISLATIVE DEVELOPMENTS

Discrimination in the public education of disabled children was commonplace in the United States until the early 1970's, when litigation and legislation guaranteed the disabled child's right to an education. Following are landmark cases which helped to establish and protect the disabled child's right to an education. Legislative developments are discussed in Chapter 2 of this almanac.

Brown v. Board of Education

In 1954, the U.S. Supreme Court handed down its decision in *Brown v. Board of Education*, 347 U.S. 483 (1954). *Brown* was a landmark civil rights case which established the principle that all children must be guaranteed an equal educational opportunity. In *Brown*, the Court found that segregated public schools were inherently unequal and deprived African-American children of equal protection under the law.

The Court stated that "it is doubtful that any child may reasonably be expected to succeed in life if he is denied the opportunity of an education. . . . [S]uch an opportunity, where the state has undertaken to provide it, is a right which must be made available to all on equal terms."

Shortly after *Brown* was decided, parents of disabled children started to file lawsuits against their school districts for segregating children with disabilities, arguing that exclusion of disabled children was also discrimination.

Mills v. Board of Education of District of Columbia

In 1972, another important decision was made in *Mills v. Board of Education of District of Columbia*, 348 F. Supp. 866 (D. DC 1972). *Mills* involved the practice of suspending, expelling and excluding "exceptional" children from the District of Columbia public schools. The Court found that the District of Columbia failed to provide publicly supported education and training to plaintiffs and other "'exceptional" children and members of their class, and excluded, suspended, reassigned, and transferred "exceptional" children from regular public school classes without affording them due process of law.

Board of Education v. Rowley

In *Board of Education v. Rowley*, 458 U.S. 176 (1982), the U.S. Supreme Court issued its first decision in a special education discrimination case. The reader is advised to refer to this decision insofar as the Court sets forth a comprehensive analysis of the evolution of special education law.

STATE EDUCATIONAL SYSTEMS

When advocating for a disabled child, it is helpful to understand the educational system under which your child's school operates, including how it works and the parties responsible for making sure it works. This chapter presents an overview of state educational systems.

Although the federal government is not responsible for funding public education, congressional enactments over the years have provided funding for programs such as vocational education, and education for disabled students. Because the U.S. Constitution does not specifically mention education as a federal government function, the general right to administer educational systems is reserved to state governments under the Tenth Amendment to the Constitution, which states:

> The powers not delegated to the United States by the Constitution, nor prohibited by it to the States, are reserved to the States respectively, or to the people.

Most of the current body of education law is derived from the states. All states have their own constitution. Although a state constitution must not conflict with the federal constitution, it may be stricter, and may provide greater rights to its people. In addition, state legislatures are constantly enacting laws dealing with education.

State laws do not have to be uniform. One state's education law can differ from that of another state. However, a state's law cannot conflict with federal law, the U.S. Constitution, or its own state constitution. Conflicts which arise concerning a state law are subject to review by the state's judiciary. If the conflict involves a state law which is inconsistent with a federal law or the U.S. Constitution, the case may be subject to federal judicial review.

Boards of Education

At the state level, a local school district—also known as a local education agency ("LEA")—is generally governed by a state governmental entity known as a Board of Education ("Board"). A Board has no inherent power or authority. Its power is generally derived from the state legislature, state constitution, and state judicial decisions. Nevertheless, Boards do have the implied power to make and enforce reasonable rules and regulations necessary for the efficient conduct of the schools. However, as set forth above, those rules and regulations must not conflict with the state statutes or constitution.

The Board is generally made up of members who are elected by the citizens of the particular district ("the board members"). In the minority of states where board members are not elected, the members are appointed to the Board by virtue of a state statute or the state constitution.

The Board is responsible for overseeing the educational process within its jurisdiction, including formulating education budgets, establishing policies and procedures, hiring certain officials, such as the superintendent of schools, and making sure that there is compliance with state and federal education laws.

Because the organizational structure, functions, powers and responsibilities of state boards of education and the entities they manage may vary from state to state, the reader is advised to check the education code of his or her jurisdiction for specific information.

A Directory of State Special Education Agencies is set forth at Appendix 3.

Intermediate School Districts

Most states have intermediate school districts which are generally an association of local school districts acting in a cooperative manner for the benefit of the entire group. Intermediate school districts are usually made up of districts which are in geographic proximity to one another. Intermediate school districts share their respective resources in order to provide certain services which individually they would not be able to undertake, such as special education programs, technical education programs, and health services.

The school district is also responsible for evaluating, at public expense, all students suspected of having disabilities from birth through twenty-one years of age, regardless of whether they attend public or private school. This function is known as "child find." Program funds are granted to public authorities, such as the local school district, who are responsible for serving eligible students, teachers, and other personnel within their boundaries, whether they attend public or private school.

School Personnel

Schools employ a variety of types of personnel, including but not limited to teachers, administrators, e.g., principals, guidance counselors, and mental health professionals. Each particular category requires some type of professional credential which demonstrates that the individual has achieved at least a minimum standard of competency in the particular profession. This is generally known as state certification which is issued by the state's department of education.

Teachers

The largest group of applicants for professional careers in education are teachers. Most states require that applicants for teaching positions complete certain prescribed academic requirements, and pass a state certification examination. Teacher certification confirms to the Board that the applicant has achieved a certain minimum level of competence and performance as a teacher. Some states require teachers to meet additional academic requirements during the course of their employment.

In general, teachers go through a period of probation until they achieve "tenure"—i.e., permanence. Once it has been demonstrated that a teacher has exhibited acceptable performance standards, he or she moves from a probationary teacher status to a permanent teacher status. However, until tenure is granted, a teacher is usually subject to periodic evaluation and dismissal. In general, once a contract period has ended, provided there is a contract, a probationary teacher may be dismissed without any recourse whatsoever.

Although dismissal is generally based on substandard performance, unless required by statute, a probationary teacher may be dismissed without any reason given for the adverse action. It is much more difficult to dismiss a teacher who has achieved tenure. There are usually specific state statutes that deal with disciplinary actions taken against tenured teachers. In general, tenured teachers can only be dismissed for "just cause."

"Just cause" implies that there is a proper reason for taking action against the tenured teacher. Although state statutes may vary, just cause may include—but is not limited to—inadequate performance evaluation; conviction of certain crimes; physical or mental incapacity; professional negligence; immorality; revocation of teacher certification; and insubordination.

Tenured teachers are also usually entitled to "due process." Due process provides procedural protections to teachers who are threatened with any adverse action, such as termination. Due process generally requires that the teacher be given an impartial hearing before the governing authority. Due process may also confer the right to appeal any adverse decision to a higher authority, such as the state court.

School Curriculum

The school curriculum generally refers to the courses a student undertakes in order to earn credit. In its broadest sense, the curriculum encompasses the entirety of educational opportunities offered by the school. In all states, the local public school is required to offer a curriculum of studies prescribed by the state.

Control over the content of the curriculum of a school district may vary among the states, according to the guidelines set forth by the particular state. Textbook selection is also subject to statute, and some states require that textbooks be chosen from an approved list compiled by the state's department of education.

Although a school may be sanctioned for noncompliance with the state mandates, the judiciary has generally recognized the implied power of the local boards of education to offer courses in addition to those mandated by the state.

CHAPTER 2:
LEGISLATIVE DEVELOPMENTS

THE REHABILITATION ACT OF 1973

The Rehabilitation Act of 1973 was enacted to protect the rights of disabled persons, in general. It is the predecessor of the Americans with Disabilities Act (the "ADA"), and served as a model for drafters of the ADA. Section 504 was intended to prevent intentional or unintentional discrimination against persons with disabilities, persons who are believed to have disabilities, or family members of persons with disabilities.

Section 504 of the Rehabilitation Act provides that qualified disabled individuals cannot be excluded from, denied the benefits of, or be subjected to discrimination under any program or activity that receives Federal financial assistance solely by reason of their handicap.

Agencies that provide Federal financial assistance also have Section 504 regulations covering entities that receive Federal aid. Because all public schools receive some type of federal assistance, Section 504 applies to public educational institutions. For educational institutions, the term "program or activity" includes any of the operations of a State educational agency (SEA) and local educational agency (LEA) receiving federal funds regardless of whether the specific program or activity involved is a direct recipient of the federal funds.

Further, the definition of a disability under Section 504 is much broader than the definition under the IDEA, which is discussed below. Thus, all children covered under the IDEA would be covered under Section 504, whereas not all children covered under Section 504 would be covered under the IDEA.

Section 504 protects all persons with a disability who:

1. Have a physical or mental impairment which substantially limits one or more major life activities;

2. Have a record of such an impairment; or

3. Are regarded as having such an impairment.

Section 504 regulations further define a "physical or mental impairment" as any physiological disorder or condition, cosmetic disfigurement or anatomical loss affecting one or more of the following body systems: (i) neurological, (ii) musculoskeletal, (iii) special sense organs, (iv) respiratory including speech organs, (v) cardiovascular, (vi) reproductive, (vii) digestive, (viii) genito-urinary, (ix) hemic and lymphatic, (x) skin or endocrine; or (xi) any mental or psychological disorder such as mental retardation, organic brain syndrome, emotional or mental illness and specific learning disabilities.

In order to be covered under Section 504, the disabled person's physical or mental impairment must have a substantial limitation on one or more major life activities, such as seeing, hearing, learning, etc. As it applies to disabled children, the issue is whether the child's impairment substantially limits his or her ability to learn.

Section 504 places responsibility on the schools to identify students with disabilities. Each school must undertake an annual investigation to identify every qualified individual with a disability residing in the school's jurisdiction who is not receiving a public education.

Section 504 requires that parents receive notice of actions regarding the identification, evaluation and placement of their children. The notice does not need to be in writing, although many districts do provide written notice so they can document the event if they are challenged. However, unlike the IDEA, there is no consent requirement under Section 504.

Selected provisions of Section 504 of the Rehabilitation Act of 1973 are set forth at Appendix 4.

THE EDUCATION FOR ALL HANDICAPPED CHILDREN ACT OF 1975 (PUBLIC LAW 94-142)

The Education for All Handicapped Children Act (the "EAHCA"), which was enacted in 1975, established the disabled child's right to a "free appropriate public education." The EAHCA was the predecessor to the Individuals with Disabilities Education Act (the "IDEA"), the primary law dealing with the education of disabled children.

Under the Act, the "free appropriate public education" is to be undertaken in the least restrictive environment appropriate to the student's individual needs. The desire to educate the disabled child in a setting which includes non-disabled children—a process known as "mainstreaming"—is emphasized, to the extent possible. The child's placement must also be in a setting which is as close to the child's home as available and appropriate, preferably in the school the child would be attending if he or she was not disabled.

Under the EAHCA, a substantial financial commitment was made by the federal government to educate learning disabled students. The Act also established a process by which State and local educational agencies may be held accountable for providing educational services for all handicapped children. Since the Act was enacted, the term "handicapped" has been replaced with the term "disabled."

THE HANDICAPPED CHILDREN'S PROTECTION ACT OF 1986

In 1986, Congress strengthened the Act by passing The Handicapped Children's Protection Act (the "HCPA"). The HCPA amended the EAHCA by awarding attorney's fees and costs to parents who are successful in litigation.

THE INDIVIDUALS WITH DISABILITIES EDUCATION ACT (PUBLIC LAW 101-476)

The Individuals with Disabilities Education Act ("IDEA") expanded upon and strengthened the provisions contained in its predecessor, the Education for All Handicapped Children Act, which was reauthorized in 1990 and retitled. The IDEA is the most significant piece of legislation affecting the educational rights of disabled children.

Selected provisions of the Individuals with Disabilities Education Act are set forth at Appendix 5.

Before the IDEA was implemented in 1975 (as the "EAHCA"), approximately 1 million disabled children were excluded from schools, and thousands more were denied appropriate services. The IDEA has changed the lives of many disabled children, who are finishing high school and attending college in unprecedented numbers.

The Individuals with Disabilities Education Act is discussed more fully in Chapter 4 of this almanac.

The IDEA reaffirms the public school's obligation to afford all eligible children with disabilities a free appropriate public education in the least restrictive environment appropriate to their individual needs, and the requirement to develop an appropriate Individualized Education Program (IEP) for each child.

Individualized Education Programs are discussed more fully in Chapter 7 of this almanac.

THE FAMILY EDUCATIONAL RIGHTS AND PRIVACY ACT OF 1974

According to the Family Educational Rights and Privacy Act ("FERPA"), schools that receive any federal funding must make student records available for viewing by parents and legal guardians, and by the students themselves provided they are age 18 or older.

Selected Provisions of the Family Educational Rights and Privacy Act are set forth at Appendix 6.

The Family Educational Rights and Privacy Act is more fully discussed in Chapter 5 of this almanac.

THE AMERICANS WITH DISABILITIES ACT OF 1990

The Americans with Disabilities Act (the "ADA") contains five titles:

1. Title I: Equal Employment Opportunity for Individuals with Disabilities—This title is designed to remove barriers that would deny qualified individuals with disabilities access to the same employment opportunities and benefits available to others without disabilities.

2. Title II: Nondiscrimination on the Basis of Disability in State and Local Government Services—This title prohibits discrimination on the basis of disability by public entities, including elementary and secondary public schools, and provides the basis for disability discrimination claims.

3. Title III: Nondiscrimination on the Basis of Disability by Public Accommodations and in Commercial Facilities—This title prohibits discrimination on the basis of disability by private entities in places of public accommodation, and requires that all new places of public accommodation and commercial facilities be designed and constructed so that they are readily accessible to, and usable by, persons with disabilities.

4. Title IV: Telecommunications—This title requires telephone companies to have developed interstate and intrastate telephone relay services in order to allow people with speech and hearing impairments who use TDDs to communicate with individuals who do not have this equipment.

5. Title V: Miscellaneous Provisions

Disability Discrimination Under Title II of the ADA

The U.S. Department of Education's Office for Civil Rights (OCR) enforces Title II in public elementary and secondary education systems and institutions, public institutions of higher education and vocational education.

Title II covers, for example, any public entertainment or lecture series a school system offers, after-school activities and social events offered by a school system, parent-teacher meetings, classroom activities, field trips or other special events, and all services provided for students or staff. Services provided by any private contractors on behalf of the school system must also comply fully with relevant provisions of Title II.

Under Title II, many of the provisions of Section 504 of the Rehabilitation Act were expanded upon. In fact, because of their similarities, both the ADA and Section 504 are administered by the Office for Civil Rights (OCR) and considered essentially identical.

Because the ADA regulations have no specific provisions regarding education programs, in interpreting the ADA, the OCR uses the standards under Section 504, except where Title II provides otherwise. The ADA statute clearly specifies, however, that unless Title II states otherwise, Title II may not be interpreted to apply a lesser degree of protection to individuals with disabilities than is provided under Section 504.

In the area of education, the federal government has stated many of the nondiscrimination requirements related to individuals with disabilities in more specific detail under Section 504 than under Title II. The reason for this difference is that the regulation issued to implement Title II was written to cover all state and local government entities regardless of their function.

On the other hand, the regulation issued under Section 504 was written to describe specific requirements applicable to public school districts, as well as certain other types of recipients of federal funds in the areas of education, health, and social services. Nevertheless, if a rule issued under Section 504 imposes a lesser standard than the ADA statute or regulation, the language in the ADA statute or regulation controls.

As it applies to disabled students, virtually every violation of Section 504 is also a violation of Title II. Thus, the OCR has stated that complaints alleging violations of one statute will automatically be investigated for violations of the other.

A sample Education Disability Discrimination Complaint is set forth at Appendix 7.

Title II prohibits discrimination against any "qualified individual with a disability." In addition, Title II also protects persons who, because of their association with persons who have disabilities, have been retaliated against for their participation in Title II activities.

Disabilities covered by Title II are limited to those that meet the ADA's legal definition—i.e., those that place substantial limitations on one or more of an individual's major life activities, and includes an individual:

(A) who has a physical or mental impairment that substantially limits one or more of the major life activities of such individual, i.e., those persons who *currently* have actual physical or mental impairments that substantially limit one or more major life activities.;

(B) who has a record of such an impairment; or

(C) who is being regarded as having such an impairment.

The phrase "major life activities" includes but is not limited to functions such as caring for one's self, performing manual tasks, walking, seeing, hearing, speaking, breathing, learning, and working.

To be considered a disability, the impairment must significantly restrict the performance of a major life activity in comparison to most people in terms of (i) conditions under which the activity is performed; (ii) the manner in which the activity is performed; or (iii) the duration of performance possible for the individual.

The finding that an impairment poses a substantial limitation is not assumed simply because an impairment exists; it is shown by determining the impact of that impairment on a particular individual. The factors that are considered in determining whether a person's impairment substantially limits a major life activity are (i) its nature and severity; (ii) its duration; and (iii) its permanent or long-term impact or expected impact.

Persons with records of physical or mental impairments includes those who have a history or record of an impairment that substantially limits a major life activity, as well as persons who have been misclassified as having an impairment.

Persons regarded as having a disability refers to people who are not, in fact, substantially limited in any major life activity but are nevertheless perceived by others as having a disability, sometimes because of myth, fear, or stereotype.

Selected provisions of the Americans with Disabilities Act are set forth at Appendix 8.

THE IMPROVING AMERICA'S SCHOOLS ACT OF 1994

The Improving America's Schools Act (IASA) reauthorized the Elementary and Secondary Education Act (ESEA), the principal federal law affecting education from kindergarten through high school, which in turn authorizes programs to benefit educationally needy elementary and secondary students living in areas with high concentrations of children from low-income families.

THE NO CHILD LEFT BEHIND ACT

On January 8, 2002, the No Child Left Behind Act (NCLB) became law. With passage of No Child Left Behind, Congress again reauthorized the Elementary and Secondary Education Act (ESEA) and implemented new programs designed to meet the educational needs of elementary and secondary students, including children with disabilities. Section 1001 of the No Child Left Behind Act sets forth its statement of purpose:

> The purpose of this title is to ensure that all children have a fair, equal, and significant opportunity to obtain a high-quality education and reach, at a minimum, proficiency on challenging State academic achievement standards and state academic assessments.

According to NCLB, this purpose can be accomplished by:

> (1) ensuring that high-quality academic assessments, accountability systems, teacher preparation and training, curriculum, and instructional materials are aligned with challenging State academic standards so that students, teachers, parents, and administrators can measure progress against common expectations for student academic achievement;

> (2) meeting the educational needs of low-achieving children in our Nation's highest-poverty schools, limited English proficient children, migratory children, children with disabilities, Indian children, neglected or delinquent children, and young children in need of reading assistance;

> (3) closing the achievement gap between high-and low-performing children, especially the achievement gaps between minority and nonminority students, and between disadvantaged children and their more advantaged peers;

> (4) holding schools, local educational agencies, and States accountable for improving the academic achievement of all students, and identifying and turning around low-performing schools that have failed to provide a high-quality education to their students, while

providing alternatives to students in such schools to enable the students to receive a high-quality education;

(5) distributing and targeting resources sufficiently to make a difference to local educational agencies and schools where needs are greatest;

(6) improving and strengthening accountability, teaching, and learning by using State assessment systems designed to ensure that students are meeting challenging State academic achievement and content standards and increasing achievement overall, but especially for the disadvantaged;

(7) providing greater decisionmaking authority and flexibility to schools and teachers in exchange for greater responsibility for student performance;

(8) providing children an enriched and accelerated educational program, including the use of schoolwide programs or additional services that increase the amount and quality of instructional time;

(9) promoting schoolwide reform and ensuring the access of children to effective, scientifically based instructional strategies and challenging academic content;

(10) significantly elevating the quality of instruction by providing staff in participating schools with substantial opportunities for professional development;

(11) coordinating services under all parts of this title with each other, with other educational services, and, to the extent feasible, with other agencies providing services to youth, children, and families; and

(12) affording parents substantial and meaningful opportunities to participate in the education of their children.

No Child Left Behind requires that all children be assessed. In order to show adequate yearly progress, schools must test at least 95 percent of the various subgroups of children, including students with disabilities. States must provide reasonable accommodations for students with disabilities.

CHAPTER 3:
THE UNITED STATES EDUCATION DEPARTMENT

IN GENERAL

The original U.S. Department of Education was created in 1867 for the purpose of gathering information that would help the states establish efficient school systems. The present U.S. Education Department ("USED") was established on May 4, 1980 by Congress by the Department of Education Organization Act.

The USED is the federal agency mainly responsible for administering federal funds for education programs, conducting education research, and enforcing federal statutes prohibiting discrimination in educational activities receiving federal funds.

MISSION

The USED's stated mission is to ensure equal access to education and to promote educational excellence throughout the nation. In achieving that goal, it assists the efforts of states and local school systems to improve the quality of education.

The USED encourages involvement of the public, parents, and students in Federal education programs; and promotes improvements in the quality and usefulness of education through Federally supported research, evaluation, and sharing of information. The USED administers more than 200 education-related programs.

ORGANIZATIONAL STRUCTURE

The USED is headquartered in Washington, D.C., and maintains ten regional offices located throughout the country. These regional offices, each directed by a Secretary's Regional Representative, provide leadership and assistance to local school systems, colleges and universities, businesses and community groups.

A directory of U.S. Education Department Regional Offices is set forth at Appendix 9.

The USED utilizes a staff of approximately 4,900 employees, most of whom are located at headquarters. One-third of the USED employees are located in the regional offices where they are primarily involved in representing USED goals within the region, particularly in the areas of student financial assistance, civil rights enforcement, and vocational rehabilitation services for the disabled.

An overview of USED programs and services is set forth below.

THE INFORMATION RESOURCE CENTER

The Information Resource Center (IRC) acts as the main entry point for telephone inquiries to the USED. The staff fulfills publication requests; provides directory information for employees, offices, and programs within the USED; and provides detailed information on the major programs and initiatives.

The IRC may be reached at 1-800-USA-LEARN. Automated services, such as fax on demand (Flashfax), Internet instructions, and audio descriptions of the USED's major programs and initiatives are available 24 hours a day, 7 days a week. Personal service is available 9 a.m. to 5 p.m. EST, Monday through Friday.

SATELLITE TOWN MEETINGS

The USED sponsors satellite town meetings made possible by telecommunications technology, where thousands of people in sites all over the country get to teleconference and discuss the most critical and timely issues in education. Renowned national experts, local educators, and community leaders participate and share ideas. Viewers may call in questions or comments to a toll free number shown on the screen during the broadcast.

Satellite town meetings are accessible through "downlinks" in local communities, or through broadcast by local cable access networks, public television stations, and major national cable outlets such as The Discovery Network and Mind Extension University. Past topics have included family and school partnerships, mathematics and science education enhancement, safer schools, charter schools, preschool programs, and connecting schools to the information superhighway Viewers can call 1-800-USA-LEARN for a listing of topics for the current school year.

THE NATIONAL LIBRARY OF EDUCATION

The National Library of Education (NLE) is the largest federally funded library in the world exclusively devoted to education. The NLE stocks more than 200,000 books and about 750 periodical subscriptions in addition to studies, reports, microfiche, CD-ROM databases, and special collections such as rare books and early American textbooks.

REGIONAL EDUCATIONAL LABORATORIES

The USED funds 10 Regional Educational Laboratories that develop materials and provide assistance to states and local educators based on the most recent knowledge about improving teaching and learning. The Regional Education Laboratories are educational research and development organizations supported by contracts with the USED's Office of Educational Research and Improvement (OERI).

The Eisenhower National Clearinghouse for Mathematics and Science Education (ENC) is one such facility which was established in 1992 at Ohio State University. ENC is the national repository for K-12 mathematics and science instructional materials and an online searchable database of those materials, as well as vast resources to support math and science education improvement.

A Directory of the USED Regional Educational Laboratories is set forth at Appendix 10.

NATIONAL EDUCATIONAL RESEARCH AND DEVELOPMENT CENTERS

To address nationally significant problems and issues in education, the OERI also supports university-based national educational research and development centers. The centers address specific topics such as early childhood development and learning, student learning and achievement, cultural and linguistic diversity and second language learning, and postsecondary improvement.

A directory of National Research & Development Centers is set forth at Appendix 11.

THE EDUCATIONAL RESOURCES INFORMATION CENTER

Since 1966, the USED's Educational Resources Information Center (ERIC) has distributed information on subjects such as early childhood education, and education for disabled and gifted children. ERIC is the world's largest database on education.

COMPETITIVE GRANT PROGRAMS

Competitive grant programs support efforts by states, school districts, postsecondary institutions, and other groups, to improve the effectiveness of education. These programs include the Fund for the Improvement of Education (FIE), and the Fund for the Improvement of Postsecondary Education (FIPSE), which sponsor innovation in elementary, secondary, and postsecondary education, and the Charter Schools program, which provides funding for the development of charter schools in states that have enacted charter school laws.

THE OFFICE OF EDUCATIONAL RESEARCH AND IMPROVEMENT

The Office of Educational Research and Improvement (OERI) funds six Regional Technology in Education Consortia under the authority of The Technology for Education Act of 1994, an amendment to Title III, Part A, Section 3141 of the Elementary and Secondary Education Act of 1965. The Regional Technology in Education Consortia program was established to help states, local educational agencies, teachers, school library and media personnel, administrators, and other education entities successfully integrate technologies into kindergarten through 12th grade classrooms, library media centers, and other educational settings, including adult literacy centers. In accomplishing its goals, the Regional Technology in Education Consortia establishes and conducts regional activities that promote the effective use of technology in education, and engages regional cooperation and resource sharing.

FINANCIAL ASSISTANCE FOR POSTSECONDARY STUDENTS

Approximately 45 percent of the USED budget is devoted to postsecondary education, most of which is used for student financial aid. Federal financial assistance for college began with the GI Bill of 1944, which provided assistance to millions of American servicemen and their families. Today, about 75 percent of all student financial aid in the nation is funded by the federal government. In order to apply for these financial aid programs, students must complete the Free Application for Federal Student Aid (FAFSA).

The Federal Pell Grant program makes grants averaging over $1,500 to nearly four million postsecondary students annually. Most Pell recipients are from families earning less than $20,000 a year.

The USED also operates two major student loan programs for which almost all students are eligible:

1. The William D. Ford Direct Loan Program—This program lends funds directly from the federal government to postsecondary stu-

dents and provides a wide variety of repayment options, including income-contingent repayment. This program has provided over $10 billion in loans at over 1,500 schools; serving more than 2.1 million student and parent borrowers since the program began.

2. The Federal Family Education Loan Program—This program provides loan subsidies and guarantees against default on loans made to students by private lenders.

Additional campus-based aid programs give postsecondary institutions great flexibility in making need-based financial assistance available to students. These programs include the low-interest Federal Perkins Loans Program; the Federal Supplemental Educational Opportunity Grant Program, which gives additional grant assistance to needy college students; and the Federal Work-Study Program, which supports mostly part-time on-campus jobs allowing 700,000 students to earn about $1,000 annually. Each of these programs requires matching funds from participating institutions.

ELEMENTARY AND SECONDARY EDUCATION

The USED delivers almost $13 billion to states and school districts for elementary and secondary education, primarily through formula-based grant programs. Under the Individuals with Disabilities Education Act (IDEA), the USED helps states and school districts meet their responsibility to provide a free appropriate public education for disabled children. The IDEA was enacted to provide a framework for appropriately serving these children as well as federal financial assistance to help pay for their education. The USED allocates nearly $3 billion under three state formula grant programs to help states meet the developmental and educational needs of over five million disabled children, from birth through age 21.

THE OFFICE OF SPECIAL EDUCATION AND REHABILITATIVE SERVICES (OSERS)

The Office of Special Education and Rehabilitative Services (OSERS) supports programs that assist in educating children with special needs, provides for the rehabilitation of youth and adults with disabilities, and supports research to improve the lives of individuals with disabilities.

The School-to-Work Opportunities Act of 1994

The School-to-Work Opportunities Act, administered jointly by the USED and the Department of Labor, provides funding to every state, and to interested communities, to develop a comprehensive school-to-work system. These systems combine school-based and work-based learning with activities designed to prepare students for their first job.

The Perkins Act Vocational Education Grant Program

The Perkins Act Vocational Education Grants help pay for vocational training programs at both the secondary and postsecondary levels. Funds may be used in accordance with state-developed plans to support activities ranging from pre-vocational courses for secondary school students to retraining adults to adapt to changing technological and labor market conditions.

The Vocational Rehabilitation Grant Program

Under the Vocational Rehabilitation Grant Program, the USED provides vocational rehabilitation grants to assist the disabled in achieving successful independent living and employment skills.

The Adult Education Act Grant Program

The Adult Education Act Grant Program helps educationally disadvantaged adults achieve literacy, certification of high school equivalency, and English language proficiency.

The Even Start Program

The Even Start Program provides formula grants to states for the support of intergenerational literacy projects combining early childhood education for children and literacy training for their parents.

OSER Departments

To carry out its functions, OSERS consists of three program-related components:

The Office of Special Education Programs (OSEP)

The Office of Special Education Programs (OSEP) has primary responsibility for administering programs and projects relating to the free appropriate public education of all children, youth and adults with disabilities, from birth through age 21. The bulk of special education funds is administered by OSEP's Monitoring and State Improvement Programs division, which provides grants to states and territories to assist them in providing a free, appropriate public education to all children with disabilities. The early intervention and preschool grant programs provide grants to each state for children with disabilities, ages birth through five.

The Rehabilitation Services Administration (RSA)

The Rehabilitation Services Administration (RSA) oversees programs that help individuals with physical or mental disabilities to obtain employment through the provision of such supports as counseling, medical and psychological services, job training, and other individualized services. The RSA's major formula grant program provides funds to state vocational rehabilitation agencies to provide employment-related services for individuals with disabilities, giving priority to individuals who are severely disabled.

National Institute on Disability and Rehabilitation Research (NIDRR)

The National Institute on Disability and Rehabilitation Research (NIDRR), provides leadership and support for a comprehensive program of research related to the rehabilitation of individuals with disabilities. Their efforts are aimed at improving the lives of individuals with disabilities from birth through adulthood.

THE OFFICE OF CIVIL RIGHTS

The Office of Civil Rights (OCR) is responsible for enforcing a variety of federal statutes prohibiting discrimination by recipients of federal education funds on the basis of race, color, national origin, gender, disability, or age. The OCR handles more than 5,000 complaints a year. More than 95 percent of these are resolved by agreement without the need for court or administrative hearing proceedings.

For assistance related to civil rights, you may contact the OCR headquarters office in Washington D.C. or the OCR enforcement office serving your state or territory. The OCR National Headquarters is located at:

U.S. Department of Education
Office for Civil Rights
Customer Service Team
550 12th Street, SW
Washington, D.C. 20202-1100
Telephone: 1-800-421-3481
TDD: 877-521-2172
FAX: 202-245-6840
E-mail: OCR@ed.gov

Filing a Complaint

When filing a discrimination complaint against an educational institution, in your letter of complaint, you must include the name of the school you are complaining about, the person who has been discriminated against, when the discrimination occurred, and you should sign and date the letter and provide contact information.

The complaint should be filed within 180 calendar days after the discrimination. Within 7 days, OCR will acknowledge receiving your complaint and will contact you by letter or telephone within 30 days to let you know whether they will proceed further with your complaint. OCR's goal is to resolve complaints within 180 days.

During the complaint process, OCR's role is to be a neutral fact-finder and resolve the complaint. The OCR has a variety of options for resolving complaints, including facilitated resolutions and investigations. The OCR does not act as an advocate for either party during the process.

The OCR does not handle cases that are being addressed by another agency or within a school's formal grievance procedure if the OCR anticipates that the agency you filed with will provide you with a resolution process comparable to the OCR process. Once the other complaint process is completed, you have 60 days to refile your complaint. The OCR's first step will be to determine whether to defer to the result reached in the other process.

The regulations under Title VI, Title IX, Section 504 and Title II do not require you to file with the OCR prior to filing a claim under these laws in Federal court. However, if you are considering filing in court, bear in mind that the OCR does not represent complaining parties or provide advice regarding court filings. You would need to use the services of your own attorney. Also, if you proceed with your claim in a court, the OCR will not continue to pursue your complaint.

THE NATIONAL CENTER FOR EDUCATION STATISTICS

The National Center for Education Statistics (NCES) is the federal entity responsible for collecting and analyzing data related to education in the United States and other nations. The NCES conducts studies, maintains statistics, and publishes reports on education activities internationally.

The NCES, along with other components of the USED Office of Educational Research and Improvement (OERI), has developed an information program that provides the users of education statistics with access to a wide range of data. Education statistics are used for a number of purposes. Congress uses them to plan federal education programs, and to apportion federal funds among the states. Federal agencies, such as the Departments of Defense, Labor, and Commerce and the National Science Foundation, use the statistics to determine the quality and supply of students coming out of our schools, and the subjects they are being taught. State and local officials use statistics for financial planning.

In addition, educational organizations, such as the American Council on Education and the National Education Association, use the statistical data for planning and research, and the news media uses education statistics to inform the public about school enrollment and expenditures.

THE UNITED STATES EDUCATION DEPARTMENT OFFICE OF NON-PUBLIC EDUCATION

The United States Education Department Office of Non-Public Education is authorized under Section 214 of the Department of Education Organization Act. The three functions of the Office of Non-Public Education are:

1. To foster maximum participation of non-public school students in all federal education programs for which they are eligible.

2. To recommend to the secretary changes in law, regulations, or policies that would increase the availability of educational services to non-public school students.

3. To review departmental programs and procedures to ensure that services for non-public school students are provided as required by law.

The Office of Non-Public Education works with the principal offices of the USED on matters of legislation, regulation, and policy when these matters concern private schools and their students, teachers, and families.

The Office of Non-Public Education is located at 600 Independence Avenue, SW, Washington, D.C. 20202-0122 Telephone: (202) 401-1365/Fax: (202) 401-1971.

CHAPTER 4:
THE INDIVIDUALS WITH DISABILITIES EDUCATION ACT ("IDEA")

IN GENERAL

The Individuals with Disabilities Education Act (IDEA) requires public schools to locate and identify children with disabilities who may be in need of specialized education. The IDEA is divided into four parts:

Part A: General Provisions, Definitions and Other Issues

Part A discusses the purpose of the special education law and includes definitions of terms that are used in the statute.

Part B: Assistance for Education of All Children with Disabilities

Part B includes funding, state plans, evaluations, eligibility, due process, discipline and other areas relating to direct services.

Part C: Infants and Toddlers with Disabilities

Part C refers to infants and children with disabilities, and defines an "at-risk infant or toddler" as an individual under 3 years of age who would be at risk of experiencing a substantial developmental delay if early intervention services were not provided.

Part D: National Activities to Improve Education of Children with Disabilities

Part D focuses on the need to improve special education programs, prepare personnel, disseminate information, supporting research, and apply research findings to education.

COVERED PERSONS

Under the IDEA, a child with a disability is defined as a child:

(1) with mental retardation; hearing impairments including deafness; speech or language impairments; visual impairments, including blindness; serious emotional disturbance; orthopedic impairments; autism; traumatic brain injury; or other health impairments, or specific learning disabilities; and

(2) who, by reason thereof, needs special education and related services.

The IDEA defines special education as specially designed instruction, at no cost to parents, to meet the unique needs of a child with a disability, including:

(1) instruction conducted in the classroom, in the home, in hospitals and institutions, and in other settings; and

(2) instruction in physical education.

A FREE APPROPRIATE PUBLIC EDUCATION

Equal educational opportunity to disabled children is achieved through the provision of a free appropriate public education (FAPE). Every qualified student with a disability is entitled to a free appropriate public education regardless of the nature or severity of their disability.

THE INDIVIDUAL EDUCATION PROGRAM (IEP)

Under the IDEA, a child who is referred for evaluation undergoes comprehensive individual testing to determine whether he or she has a disability eligible for special education and related support services. If the child is deemed eligible for special education, public school systems are required to develop appropriate Individualized Education Programs (IEPs) for the child, which must be reviewed annually.

The Individualized Education Program is discussed more fully in Chapter 7 of this almanac.

The law mandates that particular procedures be followed in the development of the IEP. The IEP must be developed by a team of knowledgeable persons, including the child's teacher; the parents, subject to certain limited exceptions; the child, if determined appropriate; an agency representative who is qualified to provide or supervise the provision of special education; and other individuals at the parents' or agency's discretion.

If parents disagree with the proposed IEP, they can request a due process hearing and review by the state educational department. They also can appeal the state agency decision to State or Federal court.

A Directory of Attorneys who Represent Parents of Children with Disabilities is set forth at Appendix 12.

THE IDEA AMENDMENTS OF 1997

In May 1997, after two years of intense analysis, discussion, legislative proposals and hearings, the U.S. House of Representatives and Senate passed legislation reauthorizing and amending the IDEA. On June 4, 1997, former President Clinton signed the bill into law. The reauthorized IDEA is called the "Individuals with Disabilities Education Act Amendments of 1997," Public Law 105-17, codified at 20 U.S.C. 1401 et seq.

The signing of the IDEA Amendments was the culmination of a process begun by the Office of Special Education and Rehabilitative Services (OSERS) in the U.S. Department of Education ("Department") in the early 1990s to review the effectiveness of the IDEA since it was first enacted in 1975 and to propose clarifications and improvements to the law in light of over two decades of experience.

Following is a summary of the IDEA Amendments of 1997 and the final regulations implementing the Amendments in 1999:

1. The least restrictive environment (LRE) requirements are maintained and strengthened in many references to educating children with disabilities. For example, children with disabilities must have access to and participate in the general education curriculum.

2. The rights of parents to be involved in educational decisions effecting their children including eligibility and placement decisions are reinforced and strengthened.

3. Challenging behavior is best approached proactively through the use of functional behavioral assessments, and positive behavior strategies, interventions and supports.

4. Children with disabilities must be included in school reform efforts as well as in state and district-wide assessments.

5. The IDEA adopted an outcome- based approach to special education; the state must establish performance goals and indicators to measure and report progress.

6. The IDEA calls on state and local agencies to engage in system-wide capacity building, linking student progress with school improvement.

The IDEA Amendments are also divided into four parts:

Part A: General Provisions

This part contains the findings and purposes of the law and the goals for the new amendments. These goals include:

1. Raising the expectations for children with disabilities and ensuring their access to the general education curriculum;

2. Strengthening the role of parents and ensuring that families have meaningful opportunities to participate in the education of their children;

3. Providing special education and related services, aids and supports in the regular classroom when appropriate; and

4. Responding to the educational needs of minority children in an increasingly diverse society.

Part A includes definitions of many of the terms used in the Act. It also clarifies the procedures regarding the U.S. Department of Education's use of policy letters and other correspondence.

Part B: Assistance for Education of All Children with Disabilities.

Part B describes the means by which the federal government will assist the states in carrying out the purposes of the Act and how the local educational agencies shall provide a free appropriate public education to students with disabilities between the ages of 3 and 21. Part B also includes the basic rights and responsibilities of children with disabilities and their parents.

PART C: INFANTS AND TODDLERS WITH DISABILITIES

Part C addresses the needs of infants and toddlers ages birth to 3 years old.

PART D: NATIONAL ACTIVITIES TO IMPROVE EDUCATION OF CHILDREN WITH DISABILITIES

Part D authorizes discretionary programs to improve the education of children with disabilities.

SIGNIFICANT CHANGES

A number of significant changes were accomplished with the enactment of the IDEA Amendments, as set forth below:

Child with a Disability

The definition of a "child with a disability" was amended to add "attention deficit disorder" and "attention deficit hyperactivity disorder" to the list of conditions that can render a child eligible for special education and related services.

The regulation clarifies that for children with ADD or ADHD, the phrase "limited strength or vitality or alertness" that defines "other health impairments" includes "a child's heightened alertness to environmental stimuli that results in limited alertness with respect to the educational environment," common characteristics of many children with ADD or ADHD.

Attention Deficit Hyperactivity Disorder is more fully discussed in Chapter 6 of this almanac.

Seriously Emotionally Disturbed

The regulations restate the change in the statute that the term "seriously emotionally disturbed" is now called "emotionally disturbed." The change in this term was not intended to have any substantive or legal significance, but was intended strictly to eliminate the pejorative connotations of the word "serious."

Parent Counseling and Training

The revised regulation adds that parent counseling and training also means "helping parents to acquire the necessary skills that will allow them to support the implementation of their child's IEP or IFSP."

A directory of Parent Training and Information Centers is set forth at Appendix 13.

Transportation

The regulations state that most children with disabilities should receive the same transportation services as non-disabled children. Further, for some children with disabilities integrated transportation may be achieved by providing needed accommodations such as lifts and other equipment or adaptations on regular school transportation vehicles.

Removals and Suspensions

A new amendment to the IDEA explicitly states that the state must ensure that a free appropriate public education (FAPE) is provided to all children with disabilities between the ages of 3 and 21, including children who have been suspended or expelled from school. The revised regulation clarifies, however, that during the first ten school days in that school year for which a child with a disability is suspended or otherwise removed from his or her placement because of a violation of school conduct rules, the school district does not need to provide services to the child with a disability if the school does not provide services to non-disabled children who have been similarly removed.

After a child has been removed from his or her current placement by school personnel for cumulatively more than 10 school days in the same school year, subsequent short term removals are permissible as long as they do not constitute a change of placement.

However, for these removals beyond ten school days, services must be provided to the extent necessary to enable the child to appropriately progress in the general curriculum and appropriately advance toward the child's IEP goals. In this situation, school personnel, in consultation with the child's special education teacher, determine the extent to which services are necessary.

Graduation

The revised regulation includes longstanding Department policy that a student's right to a FAPE is terminated upon graduation with a regular high school diploma. Graduation from high school with a regular diploma is considered a change in placement and the school must give prior written notice. However, the statutory provision which requires re-evaluation before any change in the child's eligibility, does not apply when the child is graduating from high school with a regular diploma.

Advancement

The revised regulation includes the longstanding Department policy that each state must ensure that a FAPE is available to any child who needs special education and related services, even though the child is advancing from grade to grade.

The Least Restrictive Environment

The amendments maintain the same Least Restrictive Environment (LRE) standard and requirements and add that a state's funding formula must not violate these requirements. The new law further strengthens the LRE requirement by requiring in the IEP an explanation of the extent to which the child will not participate with non-disabled children in academic, non-academic and extracurricular activities.

The statute also includes a new definition for "supplementary aids and services" which includes a range of services provided in regular education classes or other settings to enable disabled children to be educated with non-disabled children to the maximum extent appropriate.

Parentally Placed Children

The new law requires parents to provide notice to the IEP team of their intent to remove the child from the public school and place their child in a private school. This notice must be provided either at the most recent IEP meeting prior to removal or in writing within 10 business days prior to removal. If the parents do not provide such notice, reimbursement of the cost of the private school may be reduced or denied.

Placement

The revised regulation states that the services provided to a child with a disability must address all of the child's identified special education and related services and must be based on educational needs and not on the child's disability category.

Assistive Technology

The revised regulation specifies that assistive technology devices and services may be considered special education, related services, or supplementary aids and services.

Assistive Technology is discussed more fully in Chapter 7 of this almanac.

Extended School Year

The revised regulation generally restates the Department's long-standing policy regarding extended school year services that such services must be provided only if a child's IEP team determines, on an individual basis, that the services are necessary for the provision of a free appropriate public education to the child. Further, an LEA may not limit extended school year services to particular categories of disability, or unilaterally limit the type, amount, or duration of those services.

Parent Participation in Eligibility and Placement Decisions

Parents are specifically included as members of the group making the decision regarding the child's eligibility for special education services and educational placement.

REEVALUATIONS

The amendments streamline the requirements regarding the reevaluation of special education students every three years. Now, at least every three years, the IEP team must review existing evaluation data on the child, and based on that review as well as input from the parents, identify what additional information, if any, is needed to determine the following:

1. Whether the child continues to have a disability and continues to need special education and related services;

2. The child's present levels of performance and educational needs; and

3. Whether additions or modifications to the special education and related services are needed to enable the child to meet the goals set out in the IEP and to participate in the general curriculum.

If the IEP team believes that it needs more information or data to address the questions above, tests and other evaluation procedures shall be conducted in order to gather the specific information needed. If the IEP team and other qualified professionals find that no additional data is needed to determine whether the child continues to be a child with a disability, the local educational agency:

1. Shall notify the child's parents of that determination and the reasons for it, and the right of the parent to request an assessment to determine if the child continues to be a child with a disability; and

2. Shall not be required to conduct such an assessment unless requested to by the parents.

PRIVATE EDUCATION UNDER THE INDIVIDUALS WITH DISABILITIES EDUCATION ACT

As the Individuals With Disabilities Education Act (IDEA) relates to private education, Part B of the Act requires states and school districts to locate, identify, and evaluate, at public expense, those students placed by their parents in private schools who are suspected of having disabilities and needing special education and related services.

School districts must also make available a "free appropriate public education" to those parentally placed students who are determined to have disabilities. A free appropriate public education is made available at a public school setting or another appropriate setting determined by the district.

The requirement to make available a free appropriate public education does not extend beyond these settings to a private school when the child with disabilities is parentally placed in that setting. However, school districts must provide parentally placed students with disabilities who are enrolled in private elementary and secondary schools a genuine opportunity for equitable participation in their special education program, and make a free appropriate public education available to each eligible disabled student if the parents return their child to the public school.

Even though Part B does not require that all parentally placed students with disabilities receive services, in designing how the school district will provide special education services to private school students with disabilities, consideration must be given to the needs of all of the private school students with disabilities and the full range of services under Part B.

School districts must consult with appropriate representatives of students enrolled in private schools in determining, among other matters, which parentally placed disabled students will receive benefits under the program, how the students' needs will be identified, the types of services to be offered, and the manner in which the services will be provided, including the site where the services are offered and how the services under Part B will be evaluated.

The Part B program benefits provided to parentally placed students with disabilities must be comparable in quality, scope, and opportunity for participation to the program benefits provided to public school students. The "comparable benefits" provision means that students in private schools must be given the same general types of services that public school students receive and these services must be of the same general quality.

Examples of services that could be provided to parentally placed students with disabilities under Part B include speech pathology, occupational therapy, physical therapy, consultations with the private school classroom teacher, and teacher training and professional development for private school personnel. Equipment and supplies also can be provided to private school students with disabilities on the premises of the private school.

CHAPTER 5:
THE FAMILY EDUCATIONAL RIGHTS AND PRIVACY ACT OF 1974

IN GENERAL

Schools maintain records of a student's academic and personal progress from kindergarten through graduation which include, among other things, grades, progress reports, psychological reports, and teacher evaluations. According to the Family Educational Rights and Privacy Act of 1974 (FERPA), schools that receive any federal funding must make student records available for viewing by parents and legal guardians, and by the students themselves provided they are age 18 or older. In some states the age is less than 18. For example, in Delaware and Massachusetts, the age is 14.

The purpose of FERPA is to establish requirements for the protection of privacy of parents and students. An educational agency or institution must give full rights under the Act to either parent, unless the agency or institution has been provided with evidence that there is a court order, state statute, or legally binding document relating to such matters as divorce, separation, or custody that specifically revokes these rights.

The educational agency or institution, or SEA or its component, must comply with a request for access to records within a reasonable period of time, but not more than 45 days after it has received the request.

CONSENT

A parent or eligible student must provide a signed and dated written consent before an educational agency or institution will disclose personally identifiable information from the student's education records. The written consent must:

    1. Specify the records that may be disclosed;

2. State the purpose of the disclosure; and

3. Identify the party or class of parties to whom the disclosure may be made.

There are people other than the student and his or her parents who may wish to view the student's records. Although the level of protection of privacy varies from state to state, schools generally have the right to release information to teachers and school officials who have a "legitimate educational interest" in the records. This may occur, e.g, if the student transfers out of the district. Despite the written consent requirement, a school may be allowed to release a student record without obtaining permission in emergency situations where the information is necessary to protect the student's health and safety, or the health and safety of the other students.

AMENDING EDUCATION RECORDS

Inaccurate or irrelevant information contained in a student's record, such as subjective remarks by teachers, may be changed or deleted from the record upon request. If a parent or eligible student believes the education records relating to the student contain information that is inaccurate, misleading, or in violation of the student's rights of privacy, he or she may ask the educational agency or institution to amend the record.

The educational agency or institution shall decide whether to amend the record as requested within a reasonable time after the agency or institution receives the request. If the educational agency or institution decides not to amend the record as requested, it shall inform the parent or eligible student of its decision and of his or her right to a hearing.

If it is determined that there is to be no change to the record, the student and his or her parents can request that a statement be added to the record which expresses disagreement with the information. The statement becomes a permanent part of the student's record and must be released any time there is a request for the record.

PSYCHIATRIC RECORDS

There are some records which a student is not able to access, including psychiatric reports and other non-educational records possessed by a counselor, doctor, or social worker. The parents are permitted to view these files. Schools must respond to any requests for the release of files within 45 days.

SUBPOENAS

If a student's school records are subpoenaed by a court order, the school must notify the child's parents before releasing the records. In some states, the school superintendent is the only one permitted to release this information. Nevertheless, the school is not permitted to release the student's records without getting the parents' permission, unless there is an emergency situation.

FEES

An educational agency or institution may charge a fee for a copy of an education record which is made for the parent or eligible student. However, an educational agency or institution may not charge a fee to search for or to retrieve the education records of a student.

LIMITATIONS

If the education records of a student contain information on more than one student, the parent or eligible student may inspect and review or be informed of only the specific information about that student.

In addition, a postsecondary institution does not have to permit a student to inspect and review education records that are financial records, including any information those records contain of the student's parents; or certain confidential letters and statements of recommendation placed in the education records of the student.

THE COMPLAINT PROCEDURE

A parent or eligible student may file a written complaint regarding any alleged violations of the Act. The complaints are filed with the Family Policy Compliance Office, U.S. Department of Education, Washington, D.C. 20202-4605.

The complaint filed must contain specific allegations of fact giving reasonable cause to believe that a violation of the Act has occurred. The complaint must be submitted to the Office within 180 days of the date of the alleged violation or of the date that the complainant knew or reasonably should have known of the alleged violation. Under certain circumstances, the Office may extend the time limit.

The Office will notify the complainant if it does not initiate an investigation of a complaint because the complaint fails to meet the requirements. If the complaint is accepted, the Office investigates to determine whether the educational agency or institution has failed to comply with the provisions of the Act.

The Office will notify the complainant and the educational agency or institution in writing if it initiates an investigation of the complaint. The notice to the educational agency or institution generally includes the substance of the alleged violation; and requests the agency or institution to submit a written response to the complaint.

Once the Office reviews the complaint and response, it may permit the parties to submit further written or oral arguments or information. Following its investigation, the Office will provide the complainant and the educational agency or institution written notice of its findings and the basis for its findings.

If the Office finds that the educational agency or institution has not complied with the Act, the notice will:

1. Include a statement of the specific steps that the agency or institution must take to comply; and

2. Provide a reasonable period of time, given all of the circumstances of the case, during which the educational agency or institution may comply voluntarily.

HEARINGS

An educational agency or institution shall give a parent or eligible student, on request, an opportunity for a hearing to challenge the content of the student's education records on the grounds that the information contained in the education records is inaccurate, misleading, or in violation of the privacy rights of the student.

The hearing must meet, at a minimum, the following requirements:

1. The educational agency or institution shall hold the hearing within a reasonable time after it has received the request for the hearing from the parent or eligible student.

2. The educational agency or institution shall give the parent or eligible student notice of the date, time, and place, reasonably in advance of the hearing.

3. The hearing may be conducted by any individual, including an official of the educational agency or institution, who does not have a direct interest in the outcome of the hearing.

4. The educational agency or institution shall give the parent or eligible student a full and fair opportunity to present evidence relevant to the issues raised. The parent or eligible student may, at their own expense, be assisted or represented by one or more individuals of his or her own choice, including an attorney.

5. The educational agency or institution shall make its decision in writing within a reasonable period of time after the hearing.

6. The decision must be based solely on the evidence presented at the hearing.

If, as a result of the hearing, the educational agency or institution decides that the information is inaccurate, misleading, or otherwise in violation of the privacy rights of the student, it shall:

1. Amend the record accordingly; and

2. Inform the parent or eligible student of the amendment in writing.

If, as a result of the hearing, the educational agency or institution decides that the information in the education record is not inaccurate, misleading, or otherwise in violation of the privacy rights of the student, it shall inform the parent or eligible student of the right to place a statement in the record commenting on the contested information in the record or stating why he or she disagrees with the decision of the agency or institution, or both.

If an educational agency or institution places a statement in the education records of a student, the agency or institution shall:

1. Maintain the statement with the contested part of the record for as long as the record is maintained; and

2. Disclose the statement whenever it discloses the portion of the record to which the statement relates.

CHAPTER 6:
TYPES OF DISABILITIES

ATTENTION DEFICIT HYPERACTIVITY DISORDER (ADHD)

Attention Deficit Hyperactivity Disorder (ADHD)—a term which is used interchangeably with Attention Deficit Disorder (ADD)—is a complex disorder which affects a considerable number of school-age children. ADHD is defined in the fourth edition of the Diagnostic and Statistical Manual (DSM-IV) of the American Psychiatric Association as "a disorder that can include a list of nine specific symptoms of inattention and nine symptoms of hyperactivity/impulsivity."

The specific DSM-IV criteria for Attention Deficit Hyperactivity Disorder are set forth at Appendix 14.

A person must exhibit several characteristics to be clinically diagnosed as having ADHD:

1. Severity—The behavior in question must occur more frequently in the child than in other children at the same developmental stage;

2. Early Onset—At least some of the symptoms must have been present prior to age 7;

3. Duration—The symptoms must also have been present for at least 6 months prior to the evaluation;

4. Impact—The symptoms must have a negative impact on the child's academic or social life; and

5. Settings—The symptoms must be present in multiple settings.

ADHD and the evaluation process under the IDEA as it relates to this specific disability is discussed more fully below.

AUTISM

Autisim is a developmental disability significantly affecting verbal and nonverbal communication and social interaction, generally evident before age 3, that adversely affects a child's educational performance. Other characteristics often associated with autism are engagement in repetitive activities and stereotyped movements, resistance to environmental change or change in daily routines, and unusual responses to sensory experiences.

DEAF-BLINDNESS

Concomitant hearing and visual impairments, the combination of which causes such severe communication and other developmental and educational problems that the student cannot be accommodated in special education programs solely for children with deafness or children with blindness.

EMOTIONAL DISTURBANCE

A condition exhibiting one or more of the following characteristics over a long period of time and to a marked degree that adversely affects a child's educational performance:

1. An inability to learn that cannot be explained by intellectual, sensory, or health factors.

2. An inability to build or maintain satisfactory interpersonal relationships with peers and teachers.

3. Inappropriate types of behavior or feelings under normal circumstances.

4. A general pervasive mood of unhappiness or depression.

5. A tendency to develop physical symptoms or fears associated with personal or school problems.

The term includes schizophrenia. The term does not apply to children who are socially maladjusted, unless it is determined that they have an emotional disturbance.

HEARING IMPAIRMENTS

An impairment in hearing, whether permanent or fluctuating, that adversely affects a child's educational performance, in the most severe case because the child is impaired in processing linguistic information through hearing.

LEARNING DISABILITIES

The Education for All Handicapped Children Act (Public Law 94-142), defines a learning disability (LD) as a "disorder in one or more of the basic psychological processes involved in understanding or using language, spoken or written, which may manifest itself in an imperfect ability to listen, think, speak, read, write, spell or do mathematical calculations."

The definition further states that LD includes perceptual handicaps, brain injury, minimal brain dysfunction, dyslexia, and developmental aphasia. According to the law, LD does not include learning problems that are primarily the result of visual, hearing, or motor handicaps; mental retardation, or environmental, cultural, or economic disadvantage. Also required is a severe discrepancy between the child's potential—as measured by IQ—and his or her current skill level—as measured by achievement tests.

It is estimated that anywhere from 1% to 30% of the general population exhibit learning disabilities, a result which appears to reflect the variations in definitions of the term "learning disabled." However, the most widely agreed upon estimate is 2% to 3%.

Students who are learning disabled may exhibit a wide range of traits, including poor reading comprehension, spoken language, writing, and reasoning ability. Hyperactivity, inattention, and perceptual coordination problems may also be associated with LD, but are not examples of LD. Other traits that may be present include a variety of symptoms of brain dysfunction, including uneven and unpredictable test performance, perceptual impairments, motor disorders, and emotional characteristics such as impulsiveness, low tolerance for frustration, and maladjustment.

MENTAL RETARDATION

Significantly subaverage general intellectual functioning, existing concurrently with deficits in adaptive behavior and manifested during the developmental period, that adversely affects a child's educational performance.

MULTIPLE DISABILITIES

Concomitant impairments (e.g., mental retardation-blindness, mental retardation-orthopedic impairment, etc.), the combination of which causes such severe educational needs that they cannot be accommodated in special education programs solely for one of the impairments. The term does not include deaf-blindness.

ORTHOPEDIC IMPAIRMENTS

A severe orthopedic impairment that adversely affects a child's educational performance. The term includes impairments caused by congenital anomaly (e.g., clubfoot, absence of some member, etc.), impairments caused by disease (e.g., poliomyelitis, bone tuberculosis, etc.), and impairments from other causes (e.g., cerebral palsy, amputations, and fractures or burns that cause contractures).

OTHER HEALTH IMPAIRMENTS

Having limited strength, vitality or alertness, including a heightened alertness to environmental stimuli, that results in limited alertness with respect to the educational environment that:

1. Is due to chronic or acute health problems such as asthma, attention deficit disorder or attention deficit hyperactivity disorder, diabetes, epilepsy, a heart condition, hemophilia, lead poisoning, leukemia, nephritis, rheumatic fever, and sickle cell anemia; and

2. Adversely affects a child's educational performance.

SPEECH OR LANGUAGE IMPAIRMENTS

A communication disorder, such as stuttering, impaired articulation, a language impairment, or a voice impairment, that adversely affects a child's educational performance.

TRAUMATIC BRAIN INJURY

An acquired injury to the brain caused by an external physical force, resulting in total or partial functional disability or psychosocial impairment, or both, that adversely affects a child's educational performance. The term applies to open or closed head injuries resulting in impairments in one or more areas, such as cognition; language; memory; attention; reasoning; abstract thinking; judgment; problem-solving; sensory, perceptual, and motor abilities; psychosocial behavior; physical functions; information processing; and speech. The term does not apply to brain injuries that are congenital or degenerative, or to brain injuries induced by birth trauma.

VISUAL IMPAIRMENTS

An impairment in vision that, even with correction, adversely affects a child's educational performance. The term includes both partial sight and blindness.

A table setting forth the number of children aged 3 through 21 in federally supported programs for the disabled, by type of disability (1976/1977-2000/2001) is set forth at Appendix 15.

ATTENTION DEFICIT HYPERACTIVITY DISORDER (ADHD)

Statistics demonstrate that about 1% to 3% of the school-aged population has the full ADHD syndrome, without symptoms of other disorders; another 5% to 10% of the school-aged population have a partial ADHD syndrome or one with other problems, such as anxiety and depression present; and another 15% to 20% of the school-aged population may show transient, subclinical, or masquerading behaviors suggestive of ADHD. Boys are about three times more likely than girls to have symptoms of ADHD.

Commonly suspected causes of ADHD have included toxins, developmental impairments, diet, injury, ineffective parenting and heredity. While there is no biological or psychological test that makes a definitive diagnosis of ADHD, a diagnosis can be made based on a clinical history of abnormality and impairment.

There are two modalities of treatment presently in use for ADHD. Psychostimulants—such as ritalin—are the most widely used medications for the management of ADHD symptoms. Behavior modification techniques have also been used to treat the behavioral symptoms of ADHD. A thorough medical examination is also important to rule out other possible causes of ADHD like symptoms.

Educational Intervention

Laws passed during the last five years have mandated educational interventions for children with ADHD. Today, modifications and special placements in public school settings are part of treatment of ADHD. It has been recognized that children with ADHD are at risk for school failure and emotional difficulties. However, early identification and intervention has demonstrated that these children can overcome many of these hurdles and achieve success.

Statistics

Statistics demonstrate that approximately 50% of children with ADHD can be taught in the regular classroom. Teachers must be trained to recognize the special needs of these students and to make any appropriate teaching and classroom modifications. The other 50% will require some degree of special education and related services.

Of this 50%, about 35-40% will primarily be served in the regular classroom with additional support, or receive some special services outside of the classroom. The most severely affected, 10-15%, may require self-contained classrooms.

ELIGIBILITY UNDER THE IDEA

In 1991, the Office of Special Education and Rehabilitative Services (OSERS) recognized that ADHD can result in significant learning problems for children with those conditions. The memorandum served to clarify the circumstances under which children with ADHD are eligible for special education services under Part B of the Individuals with Disabilities Education Act.

During the reauthorization of the IDEA, Congress gave serious consideration to including ADHD in the definition of "children with disabilities" in the statute. OSERS took the position that ADHD does not need to be added as a separate disability category in the statutory definition since children with ADHD who require special education and related services can meet the eligibility criteria for services under Part B of the IDEA.

The list of chronic or acute health problems included within the definition of "other health impaired" in the Part B regulations is not exhaustive. The term "other health impaired" includes chronic or acute impairments that result in limited alertness, which adversely affects educational performance. Thus, children with ADHD should be classified as eligible for services under the "other health impaired" category in instances where the ADHD is a chronic or acute health problem that results in limited alertness, which adversely affects educational performance.

In other words, children with ADHD, where the ADHD is a chronic or acute health problem resulting in limited alertness, may be considered disabled under Part B solely on the basis of this disorder within the "other health impaired" category in situations where special education and related services are needed because of the ADHD.

Children with ADHD are also eligible for services under Part B if the children satisfy the criteria applicable to other disability categories. For example, children with ADHD are also eligible for services under the "specific learning disability" category of Part B if they meet the criteria stated in the regulations, or under the "emotionally disturbed" category of Part B if they meet the criteria.

Evaluation

As set forth in Chapter 1, school districts have an affirmative obligation to evaluate a child who is suspected of having a disability to determine the child's need for special education and related services. The school district may not refuse to evaluate the possible need for special education and related services of a child with a prior medical diagnosis of ADHD solely by reason of that medical diagnosis. However, a medical diagnosis of ADHD alone is not sufficient to render a child eligible for services under Part B.

Under Part B, before any action is taken with respect to the initial placement of a child with a disability in a program providing special education and related services, a full and individual evaluation of the child's educational needs must be conducted in accordance with requirements of the regulations. A child's evaluation must be conducted by a multidisciplinary team, including at least one teacher or other specialist with knowledge in the area of suspected disability.

An evaluation for ADHD will often include assessment of intellectual, academic, social and emotional functioning, including gathering data from teachers as well as other adults who may interact on a routine basis with the child being evaluated. School is often where the characteristics of ADHD are first noted because the school setting requires the very skills that are difficult for these children, such as sustained attention to a task.

School districts must ensure that children with ADHD who are determined eligible for services under Part B receive special education and related services designed to meet their unique needs, including special education and related services needs arising from the ADHD. A full continuum of placement alternatives, including the regular classroom, must be available for providing special education and related services required in the IEP.

CHAPTER 7:
EDUCATING THE SPECIAL NEEDS CHILD

THE SPECIAL EDUCATION PROCESS

There are a number of basic steps that must be taken in order to identify, evaluate and determine the eligibility of a child in need of special
education and related services, and initiate those services, as set forth
below.

Child Find

In order to identify, locate, and evaluate all children with disabilities in
the state who need special education and related services, the state
must conduct "Child Find" activities. A child may be identified by
"Child Find," and parents may be asked if the "Child Find" system can
evaluate their child. Parents can also call the "Child Find" system and
ask that their child be evaluated. In other cases, the school professional may ask that a child be evaluated to see if he or she has a disability. Parents may also contact the child's teacher or other school
professional to ask that their child be evaluated. This request may be
verbal or in writing.

The Evaluation

Parental consent is needed before the child may be evaluated, and the
evaluation needs to be completed within a reasonable time after the
parent gives consent. The evaluation must assess the child in all areas
related to the child's suspected disability. The evaluation results are
used to decide the child's eligibility for special education and related
services and to make decisions about an appropriate educational program for the child. If the parents disagree with the evaluation, they
have the right to take their child for an Independent Educational Evaluation (IEE), and can ask that the school system pay for this IEE.

The Eligibility Decision

A group of qualified professionals, along with the parents, look at the child's evaluation results. They decide if the child is a "child with a disability," as defined by the IDEA. Parents may ask for a hearing to challenge the eligibility decision. If the child is found to be a "child with a disability," as defined by IDEA, he or she is eligible for special education and related services.

The IEP Meeting

Within 30 calendar days after a child is determined eligible, the team of professionals must meet to write an Individualized Education Program (IEP) for the child. The school system must schedule and conduct the IEP meeting. School staff must:

1. Contact the participants, including the parents;

2. Notify parents early enough to make sure they have an opportunity to attend;

3. Schedule the meeting at a time and place agreeable to parents and the school;

4. Tell the parents the purpose, time, and location of the meeting;

5. Tell the parents who will be attending; and

6. Tell the parents that they may invite people to the meeting who have knowledge or special expertise about the child.

At the meeting, the IEP team discusses the child's needs and writes the IEP. Parents—and the student, if appropriate—are part of the team.

Consent

Before the school system may provide special education and related services to the child for the first time, the parents must give consent. The child begins to receive services as soon as possible after the meeting. If the parents do not agree with the IEP and placement, they may discuss their concerns with other members of the IEP team and try to work out an agreement. If they still disagree, parents can ask for mediation, or the school may offer mediation. Parents may also file a complaint with the state education agency and may request a due process hearing, at which time mediation must be available.

Services

The school is obligated to make sure that the child's IEP is being carried out as it was written. Parents are given a copy of the IEP. Each of the child's teachers and service providers has access to the IEP and knows his or her specific responsibilities for carrying out the IEP. This includes the accommodations, modifications, and supports that must be provided to the child, in keeping with the IEP.

Progress Reports

The child's progress toward the annual goals is measured, as stated in the IEP. His or her parents are regularly informed of their child's progress and whether that progress is enough for the child to achieve the goals by the end of the year. These progress reports must be given to parents at least as often as parents are informed of a nondisabled children's progress.

Annual Review

The child's IEP is reviewed by the IEP team at least once a year, or more often if the parents or school ask for a review. If necessary, the IEP is revised. Parents, as team members, must be invited to attend these meetings. Parents can make suggestions for changes, can agree or disagree with the IEP goals, and agree or disagree with the placement.

If parents do not agree with the IEP and placement, they may discuss their concerns with other members of the IEP team and try to work out an agreement. As with the initial placement, if they still disagree, parents can ask for mediation, or file a complaint with the state education agency and request a due process hearing.

Reevaluation

At least every three years the child must be reevaluated. This evaluation is often called a "triennial." Its purpose is to find out if the child continues to be a "child with a disability," as defined by IDEA, and what the child's educational needs are. However, the child must be reevaluated more often if conditions warrant or if the child's parent or teacher asks for a new evaluation.

Stay Put Provision

Under the law, a child is required to remain in his or her current IEP placement pending any proposed changes or opposition to the placement. This is known as the "stay put" provision. Because the review process can be lengthy and time-consuming, parents who disagree with their child's placement sometimes unilaterally, at their own expense, place their child in another program without first obtaining consent. The parents then seek reimbursement of the expenses from the school district. However, if the courts determine that the child's IEP was appropriate, reimbursement will be denied.

THE INDIVIDUALIZED EDUCATION PROGRAM

The Individualized Education Program (IEP) is a very important document for children with disabilities, and for those who are involved in educating them. Each child's IEP describes, among other things, the educational program that has been designed to meet that child's unique needs. Each child's IEP is different and is prepared for that child alone. The IEP must include certain information about the child and the individualized education program designed to meet his or her unique needs, as follows:

Current Performance

The IEP must state how the child is currently doing in school, known as present levels of educational performance. This information usually comes from results of classroom tests and assignments, individual tests given to decide eligibility for services or during reevaluation, and observations made by parents, teachers, related service providers, and other school staff. The statement about "current performance" includes how the child's disability affects his or her involvement and progress in the general curriculum.

Annual Goals

Annual goals refers to those goals that the child can reasonably accomplish in a year. The goals are broken down into short-term objectives or benchmarks. Goals may be academic, address social or behavioral needs, relate to physical needs, or address other educational needs. The goals must be measurable, i.e., it must be possible to measure whether the student has achieved the goals.

Special Education and Related Services

The IEP must list the special education and related services to be provided to the child or on behalf of the child. This includes supplementary aids and services that the child needs. It also includes modifications to the program or supports for school personnel—such as training or professional development—that will be provided to assist the child.

Participation with Nondisabled Children

The IEP must explain the extent, if any, to which the child will not participate with nondisabled children in the regular class and other school activities.

Participation in State and District Tests

Most states and districts give achievement tests to children in certain grades or age groups. The IEP must state what modifications in the administration of these tests the child will need. If a test is not appropriate for the child, the IEP must state why the test is not appropriate and how the child will be tested instead.

Dates and Places of Services

The IEP must state when services will begin, how often they will be provided, where they will be provided, and how long they will last.

Need for Transition Services

Beginning when the child is age 14, the IEP must address the courses he or she needs to take to reach his or her post-school goals. A statement of the need for transition services must also be included in each of the child's subsequent IEPs. Beginning when the child is age 16 (or younger) the IEP must state what transition services are needed to help the child prepare for leaving school.

Beginning at least one year before the child reaches the age of majority, the IEP must include a statement that the student has been told of any rights that will transfer to him or her at the age of majority. However, this statement would be needed only in states that transfer rights at the age of majority.

Progress

The IEP must state how the child's progress will be measured and how parents will be informed of that progress.

A sample Individualized Education Program is set forth at Appendix 16.

THE IEP TEAM MEMBERS

The law requires that certain individuals be involved in writing a child's IEP. An IEP team member may fill more than one of the team positions. if properly qualified and designated. For example, the school system representative may also be the person who can interpret the child's evaluation results. IEP team members include:

Parents

Parents are key members of the IEP team because they know their child very well and can talk about their child's strengths and needs, as well as their ideas for enhancing their child's education. If the parents are deaf or have limited proficiency in the English language, the school district must make reasonable efforts to arrange for an interpreter to be present at the IEP meeting so that the parents are able to participate fully in the process.

Teachers

Teachers are vital participants in the IEP meeting as well. At least one of the child's regular education teachers must be on the IEP team if the child is participating in the regular education environment. The child's special education teacher is also a member of the team and contributes important information and experience about how to educate children with disabilities.

The special education teacher also has the responsibility for working with the student to carry out the IEP. He or she may work with the student in a resource room or special class devoted to students receiving special education services; team teach with the regular education teacher; and/or work with other school staff, e.g., the regular education teacher, to provide expertise about addressing the child's unique needs.

Individual Interpreting Evaluation Results

Another important member of the IEP team is the individual who can interpret what the child's evaluation results mean in terms of designing appropriate instruction. The evaluation results are very useful in determining how the child is currently doing in school and the child's areas of need.

Individual Representing the School System

The individual representing the school system is the team member who knows a great deal about special education services and educating children with disabilities, and can discuss the necessary school resources. It is important that this individual have the authority to commit resources and be able to ensure that whatever services are set out in the IEP will actually be provided.

Related Services Professionals

The IEP team may also include additional individuals with knowledge or special expertise about the child. The parents or the school system can invite these individuals to participate on the team. Parents, for example, may invite an advocate who knows the child, or a professional with special expertise about the child and his or her disability, who can talk about the child's strengths and/or needs. The school system may invite one or more individuals who can offer special expertise or knowledge about the child, such as a paraprofessional or related services professional.

Because an important part of developing an IEP is considering a child's need for related services, related service professionals are often involved as IEP team members or participants. They share their special expertise about the child's needs and how their own professional services can address those needs. Depending on the child's individual needs, some related service professionals attending the IEP meeting or otherwise helping to develop the IEP may include occupational or physical therapists, psychologists, or speech-language pathologists.

The Student

The student may also be a member of the IEP team. If transition services are going to be discussed at the meeting, the student must be invited to attend.

RELATED SERVICES

A child may require related services in order to benefit from special education. Related services, as listed under IDEA, include, but are not limited to:

1. Audiology services;

2. Counseling services;

3. Early identification and assessment of disabilities in children;

4. Medical services;

5. Occupational therapy;

6. Orientation and mobility services;

7. Parent counseling and training;

8. Physical therapy;

9. Psychological services;

10. Recreation;

11. Rehabilitation counseling services;

12. School health services;

13. Social work services in schools;

14. Speech-language pathology services; and

15. Transportation.

If a child needs a particular related service in order to benefit from special education, the related service professional should be involved in developing the IEP. He or she may be invited by the school or parent to join the IEP team as a person "with knowledge or special expertise about the child."

SPECIAL FACTORS

Depending on the needs of the child, the IEP team needs to consider what the law calls "special factors," as follows:

Behavior

If the child's behavior interferes with his or her learning or the learning of others, the IEP team will consider strategies and supports to address the child's behavior.

English Proficiency

If the child has limited proficiency in English, the IEP team will consider the child's language needs as these needs relate to his or her IEP.

Blindness or Visual Impairment

If the child is blind or visually impaired, the IEP team must provide for instruction in Braille or the use of Braille, unless it determines after an appropriate evaluation that the child does not need this instruction.

Communication Needs

If the child has communication needs, the IEP team must consider those needs. For example, if the child is deaf or hearing impaired, the IEP team will consider his or her language and communication needs. This includes the child's opportunities to communicate directly with classmates and school staff in his or her usual method of communication, e.g., sign language.

Assistive Technology

The IEP team must also consider the child's need for assistive technology devices or services. Assistive technology devices and services or discussed more fully below.

PLACEMENT DECISIONS

The decision regarding a child's placement is made by a group of people who know the child, can interpret the evaluation results, and are familiar with appropriate types of placement. In some states, the IEP team serves as the group making the placement decision. In other states, this decision may be made by another group of people. In all cases, the parents have the right to be members of the group that decides the educational placement of the child.

Depending on the needs of the child, his or her IEP may be carried out in the regular class with supplementary aids and services, as needed; in a special class, where every student in the class is receiving special education services for some or all of the day; in a special school; at home; in a hospital or institution; or in another appropriate setting.

Nevertheless, placement decisions must be made according to IDEA's least restrictive environment (LRE) requirements. These requirements state that, to the maximum extent appropriate, children with disabilities must be educated with children who do not have disabilities, also known as "mainstreaming." Removal of children with disabilities from the regular educational environment may occur only if the nature or severity of the child's disability is such that education in regular classes with the use of supplementary aids and services cannot be achieved satisfactorily.

Since 1988, studies have shown that U.S. schools have found the regular education classroom to be the "least restrictive environment" for increasing numbers of students with disabilities. In 1998–99, states reported that 47 percent of students with disabilities spent 80 percent or more of the day in a regular education classroom whereas in 1988–89, only 31 percent of such students did so.

A table setting forth the percentage of disabled persons aged 6 through 21 receiving education services, by age group and educational environment (1998-1999) is set forth at Appendix 17.

The increase in the percentage of students with disabilities included in regular classrooms is particularly noteworthy because the number of such students has been growing faster than total school enrollments. The ratio of special education students to total K–12 enrollment in 1988–89 was 112 per 1,000 students compared to 130 per 1,000 students in 1998–99.

Although the percentage of students with disabilities placed in regular classrooms for at least 80 percent of the day increased between 1988–89 and 1998–99, the size of increase varied by type of disability. The largest increase occurred among students with specific learning disabilities (from 20 to 45 percent). The smallest increases occurred among students with multiple disabilities (from 7 to 11 percent) and those who are both deaf and blind (from 12 to 14 percent). The percentage of students with disabilities educated in separate facilities declined for students of all disability types except for those with visual impairments.

ACCESS TO THE IEP

After the IEP has been written, parents must receive a copy at no cost. The IDEA also states that everyone who will be involved in implementing the IEP must have access to the document including: (1) regular education teacher(s); (2) special education teacher(s); (3) related service provider(s); and (4) any other service provider responsible for a part of the child's education.

Each of these individuals needs to know what his or her specific responsibilities are for carrying out the child's IEP. This includes the specific accommodations, modifications, and supports that the child must receive, according to the IEP.

A directory of information sources about special education and the IEP process is set forth at Appendix 18.

TRANSITION SERVICES

Transition refers to activities meant to prepare students with disabilities for adult life. This can include developing postsecondary education and career goals, getting work experience while still in school, setting up linkages with adult service providers such as the vocational rehabilitation agency—whatever is appropriate for the student, given his or her interests, preferences, skills, and needs. As set forth above, statements about the student's transition needs must be included in the IEP after the student reaches a certain age.

ASSISTIVE TECHNOLOGY

As set forth above, a child's IEP must set forth any assistive technology devices or services that the child requires as part of their special education and related services. Assistive technology refers to any kind of technology that can be used to help a disabled person become more independent. The Individuals with Disabilities Education Act (IDEA) sets forth the school district's responsibility to provide assistive technology to students with disabilities if it is determined by an IEP team that the child needs it to benefit from his or her educational program. In addition, a child is allowed to take an assistive technology device home if it is needed to enable him or her to benefit from his educational program as determined the IEP team.

In order to determine whether a child needs assistive technology, an assessment should be undertaken where different types of technology are introduced to the child. If it is determined that the child would benefit from the device, selection of the device, and training in its use, should begin for the child and any other individuals who are involved with the child's development, including family, service providers, and teachers.

SCHOOL DISCIPLINE FOR DISABLED CHILDREN

Prior to the 1975 amendments to the Education of the Handicapped Act (EHA)—predecessor to the IDEA, the special educational needs of children with disabilities were not being met. School officials often used disciplinary measures to exclude disabled children from education simply because they were different or more difficult to educate than nondisabled children. When the IDEA was reauthorized in 1997, Congress recognized that in certain instances school districts needed increased flexibility to deal with safety issues while maintaining needed due process protections for these children.

The protections set forth in the IDEA regarding discipline are designed to prevent speculative and subjective decision making by school officials that led to widespread abuses of the rights of children with disabilities to an appropriate education in the past, e.g., where children are excluded entirely from education because they were identified as having a behavior problem.

The discipline provisions of the IDEA allow responsible and appropriate changes in placement of children with disabilities *when their parents do not object*. If school officials believe that a child's placement is inappropriate they can work with the child's parent through the IEP and placement processes to come up with an appropriate placement for the child that will meet the needs of the child and result in his or her improved learning and the learning of others and ensure a safe environment.

If a child has behavior problems that interfere with his or her learning or the learning of others, or commits an infraction that is not considered serious, schools can address the misconduct through appropriate instructional and/or related services, including conflict management, behavior management strategies, and measures, such as time-outs and restrictions in privileges, so long as they are not inconsistent with the child's IEP. If the IEP team determines that such services are needed, they must be added to the IEP and must be provided to the child.

Disciplinary Removal from Regular Placement

The provisions of the IDEA concerning the amount of time a child with a disability can be removed from his or her regular placement for disciplinary reasons only apply if the removal constitutes a change of placement and the *parents object* to the proposed action by school officials and request a due process hearing. These discipline rules are exceptions to the generally applicable requirement that a child remains in his or her current placement during the pendency of due process, and subsequent judicial proceedings.

Even if the parents do not agree, school officials can generally remove any child with a disability from his or her regular school placement for up to 10 school days at a time whenever discipline is appropriate and is administered consistent with the treatment of nondisabled children. However, school officials cannot use this authority to repeatedly remove a child from his or her current placement if that series of removals means the child is removed for more than 10 school days in a school year, and factors such as the length of each removal, the total amount of time that the child is removed, and the proximity of the removals to one another lead to the conclusion that there has been a change in placement.

Beginning on the eleventh cumulative day in a school year that a child with a disability is removed from his or her current placement, the school district must provide those services determined to be necessary to enable the child to appropriately progress in the general curriculum and appropriately advance toward achieving the goals set out in the child's IEP. School personnel would determine where those services would be provided. This means that for the remainder of the removal that includes the eleventh day, and for any subsequent removals, services must be provided to the extent determined necessary, while the removal continues.

Further, within 10 business days after removing a child with a disability for more than 10 cumulative school days in a school year, the school district must convene an IEP team meeting to develop a behavioral assessment plan if the district has not already conducted a functional behavioral assessment and implemented a behavioral intervention plan for the child.

If the IEP team concludes that the child's behavior was not a manifestation of the child's disability, the child can be disciplined in the same manner as nondisabled children, except that appropriate educational services must be provided. This means that if nondisabled children are long-term suspended or expelled for a particular violation of school rules, the child with disabilities may also be long-term suspended or expelled.

Discipline for Weapon and Drug Offenses

School authorities can also unilaterally remove a disabled child from their regular placement for up to 45 days at a time if the child has brought a weapon to school or to a school function, or knowingly possessed or used illegal drugs or sold or solicited the sale of controlled substances while at school or a school function. In addition, if school officials believe that a child with a disability is substantially likely to injure himself or others in the child's regular placement, they can ask an impartial hearing officer to order that the child be removed to an interim alternative educational setting for a period of up to 45 days.

If at the end of an interim alternative educational placement of up to 45 days, school officials believe that it would be dangerous to return the child to the regular placement because the child would be substantially likely to injure himself or others in that placement, they can ask an impartial hearing officer to order that the child remain in an interim alternative educational setting for an additional 45 days. If necessary, school officials can also request subsequent extensions of these interim alternative educational settings for up to 45 days at a time if school officials continue to believe that the child would be substantially likely to injure himself or others if returned to his or her regular placement.

Additionally, at any time, school officials may seek to obtain a court order to remove a child with a disability from school or to change a child's current educational placement if they believe that maintaining the child in the current educational placement is substantially likely to result in injury to the child or others.

Finally, school officials can report crimes committed by children with disabilities to appropriate law enforcement authorities to the same extent as they do for crimes committed by nondisabled students.

APPENDIX 1:
AGES FOR COMPULSORY SCHOOL ATTENDANCE, BY STATE

STATE	AGE
Alabama	7 to 16
Alaska	7 to 16
Arizona	6 to 16
Arkansas	5 to 17
California	6 to 18
Colorado	7 to 16
Connecticut	7 to 16
Delaware	5 to 16
District of Columbia	5 to 18
Florida	6 to 18
Georgia	6 to 16
Hawaii	6 to 18
Idaho	7 to 16
Illinois	7 to 16
Indiana	7 to 18
Iowa	6 to 16
Kansas	7 to 18
Kentucky	6 to 16
Louisiana	7 to 17
Maine	7 to 17
Maryland	5 to 16
Massachusetts	6 to 16
Michigan	6 to 16
Minnesota	7 to 18

STATE	AGE
Mississippi	6 to 17
Missouri	7 to 16
Montana	7 to 16
Nebraska	7 to 16
Nevada	7 to 17
New Hampshire	6 to 16
New Jersey	6 to 16
New Mexico	5 to 18
New York	6 to 16
North Carolina	7 to 16
North Dakota	7 to 16
Ohio	6 to 18
Oklahoma	5 to 18
Oregon	7 to 18
Pennsylvania	8 to 17
Rhode Island	6 to 16
South Carolina	5 to 16
South Dakota	6 to 16
Tennessee	6 to 17
Texas	6 to 18
Utah	6 to 18
Vermont	7 to 16
Virginia	5 to 18
Washington	8 to 18
West Virginia	6 to 16
Wisconsin	6 to 18
Wyoming	6 to 16

Source: U.S. Department of Labor.

APPENDIX 2:
COMPULSORY SPECIAL EDUCATION SERVICES FOR STUDENTS, BY STATE AND AGE RANGE

STATE	AGE
Alabama	6 to 21
Alaska	3 to 22
Arizona	3 to 22
Arkansas	5 to 21
California	Birth to 21
Colorado	3 to 21
Connecticut	Under 21
Delaware	3 to 20
District of Columbia	n/a
Florida	n/a
Georgia	Under 21
Hawaii	Under 20
Idaho	3 to 21
Illinois	3 to 212
Indiana	3 to 22
Iowa	Under 21
Kansas	School age
Kentucky	Under 21
Louisiana	3 to 21
Maine	5 to 19
Maryland	Under 21
Massachusetts	3 to 21

STATE	AGE
Michigan	Under 26
Minnesota	Under 22
Mississippi	Birth to 20
Missouri	Under 21
Montana	3 to 18
Nebraska	Birth to 21
Nevada	Under 22
New Hampshire	3 to 21
New Jersey	5 to 21
New Mexico	School age or as provided by law
New York	Under 21
North Carolina	5 to 20
North Dakota	3 to 20
Ohio	Under 22
Oklahoma	3 and up
Oregon	3 to 21
Pennsylvania	6 to 21
Rhode Island	3 to 21
South Carolina	3 to 21
South Dakota	Under 21
Tennessee	3 to 21
Texas	3 to 21
Utah	3 to 22
Vermont	3 to 21
Virginia	2 to 21
Washington	3 to 21
West Virginia	5 to 21
Wisconsin	Under 21
Wyoming	3 to 21

NOTES:

1. n/a = not available

Source: Council of Chief State School Officers.

APPENDIX 3:
DIRECTORY OF STATE SPECIAL EDUCATION AGENCIES

STATE	DEPARTMENT	ADDRESS	TELEPHONE	FAX
ALABAMA	Alabama Department of Education, Division of Special Education Services	50 North Ripley Street Gordon Persons Building Montgomery, AL 36130-3901	334-242-8114	334-242-9192
ALASKA	Alaska Department of Education, Office of Special & Supplemental Services	801 West Tenth Street, Suite 200 Juneau, AK 99801-1894	907-465-2971	907-465-3396
ARIZONA	Arizona Department of Education, Special Education Office	1535 West Jefferson Phoenix, AZ 85007-3280	602-542-3084	602-542-5404
ARKANSAS	Arkansas Department of Education, Special Education Office	State Capitol Mall, Room 105-C #4 Little Rock, AR 72201-1071	501-682-4221	501-682-4313
CALIFORNIA	California Department of Education, Special Education Office	515 L Street, #270 Sacramento, CA 95814	916-445-4602	916-327-3706

STATE	DEPARTMENT	ADDRESS	TELEPHONE	FAX
COLORADO	Colorado Department of Education, Special Education Services Unit	201 East Colfax Avenue Denver, CO 80203	303-866-6697	303-866-6811
CONNECTICUT	Connecticut State Department of Education, Bureau of Special Education & Pupil Personnel Services	25 Industrial Park Road Middletown, CT 06457	860-638-4000	860-638-4156
DISTRICT OF COLUMBIA	D.C. State Office of Special Education	Goding School 10th and F Streets NE Washington, DC 20002	202-724-7833	202-724-5116
DELAWARE	Delaware Department of Public Instruction, Exceptional Children Team	PO Box 1402 Dover, DE 19903-1402	302-739-5471	302-739-2388
FLORIDA	Florida Department of Education, Bureau for Exceptional Students	Florida Education Center 325 West Gaines Street, Suite 614 Tallahassee, FL 32399-0400	904-488-1570	904-487-2194
GEORGIA	Georgia Department of Education, Division for Exceptional Students	1952 Twin Towers East 205 Butler Street Atlanta, GA 39334-5040	404-656-3963	404-651-6457
HAWAII	Hawaii Department of Education, Special Education Section	3430 Leahi Avenue Honolulu, HI 96815	808-733-4990	808-773-4841
IDAHO	Idaho State Department of Education, Special Education Section	650 West State Street Boise, ID 83720-3650	208-334-3940	208-334-4664

STATE	DEPARTMENT	ADDRESS	TELEPHONE	FAX
ILLINOIS	Illinois State Board of Education, Center on Policy, Planning and Resource Management	Mail Code E-284 100 North First Street Springfield, IL 62777-0001	217-782-3371	217-524-7784
INDIANA	Indiana Department of Education, Division of Special Education	State House, Room 229 Indianapolis, IN 46204-2798	317-232-0570	317-232-0589
IOWA	Iowa Department of Public Instruction, Bureau of Special Education	Grimes State Office Building Des Moines, IA 50319-0146	515-281-3176	515-242-6019
KANSAS	Kansas State Board of Education, Special Education Outcomes Team	120 SE 10th Avenue Topeka, KS 66612-1182	913-296-3869	913-296-7933
KENTUCKY	Kentucky Department of Education, Division of Exceptional Children Services	500 Mero Street, Room 805 Frankfort, KY 40601	502-564-4970	502-564-6721
LOUISIANA	Louisiana Department of Education, Office of Special Education Services	P.O. Box 94064, 9th Floor Baton Rouge, LA 70804-9064	504-342-3633	504-342-5880
MARYLAND	Maryland Department of Education, Division of Special Education	200 West Baltimore Street Baltimore, MD 21201-2595	410-767-0238	410-333-8165
MAINE	Maine Department of Education, Division of Special Education	Station #23 Augusta, ME 04333	207-287-5950	207-287-5900

STATE	DEPARTMENT	ADDRESS	TELEPHONE	FAX
MASSACHUSETTS	Massachusetts Department of Education, Educational Improvement Group	350 Main Street Malden, MA 02148-5023	617-388-3300	617-388-3394
MICHIGAN	Michigan Department of Education, Special Education Services	P.O. Box 30008 Lansing, MI 48909-75208	517-373-9433	517-373-7504
MINNESOTA	Minnesota Department of Education, Special Education Section	812 Capitol Square Building 550 Cedar Street St Paul, MN 55101-2233	612-296-1793	612-297-7368
MISSISSIPPI	Mississippi State Department of Education, Bureau of Special Services	P.O. Box 771 Jackson, MS 39205-0771	601-359-3490	601-359-2326
MISSOURI	Missouri Department of Elementary & Secondary Education, Special Education Programs	P.O. Box 480 Jefferson City, MO 65102-0480	573-751-2965	573-526-4404
MONTANA	Montana Office of Public Instruction, Division of Special Education	State Capitol, Room 106 Helena, MT 59620	406-444-4429	406-444-3924
NEBRASKA	Nebraska Department of Education, Special Education Office	301 Centennial Mall South P.O. Box 94987 Lincoln, NE 68509-4987	402-471-2471	402-471-0117
NEVADA	Nevada Department of Education, Special Education Branch	440 West King Capitol Complex Carson City, NV 89710-0004	702-687-9142	702-687-9123

STATE	DEPARTMENT	ADDRESS	TELEPHONE	FAX
NEW HAMPSHIRE	New Hampshire Department of Education, Special Education Services	101 Pleasant Street Concord, NH 03301-3860	603-271-6693	603-271-1953
NEW JERSEY	New Jersey Department of Education, Office of Special Education Programs	CN 500 Trenton, NJ 08625-0001	609-633-6833	609-984-8422
NEW MEXICO	New Mexico State Department of Education, Special Education Department	300 Don Gaspar Avenue Santa FE, NM 87501-2786	505-827-6541	505-827-6791
NEW YORK	New York State Education Department, Office for Special Education Services	One Commerce Plaza Room 1901 99 Washington Avenue Albany, NY 12234-0001	518-474-5548	518-473-5387
NORTH CAROLINA	North Carolina Department of Public Instruction, Division of Exceptional Childrens Services	301 North Wilmington Street Raleigh, NC 27601-2825	919-715-1565	919-715-1569
NORTH DAKOTA	North Dakota Department of Public Instruction, Special Education Department	600 East Boulevard Bismarck, ND 58505-0440	701-328-2277	701-328-2461
OHIO	Ohio Department of Education, Division of Special Education	933 High Street Worthington, OH 43085-4087	614-466-2650	614-728-1097
OKLAHOMA	Oklahoma State Department of Education, Special Education Section	2500 North Lincoln Boulevard Oklahoma City, OK 73105-4599	405-521-4868	405-522-3503

STATE	DEPARTMENT	ADDRESS	TELEPHONE	FAX
OREGON	Oregon Department of Education, Office of Special Education	255 Capitol Street NE Salem, OR 97310-0203	503-378-3598	503-373-7968
PENNSYLVANIA	Pennsylvania Department of Education, Bureau of Special Education	333 Market Street Harrisburg, PA 17126-0333	717-783-6913	717-783-6139
RHODE ISLAND	Rhode Island Department of Education, Office of Special Needs	Shepard Building 225 Westminster Street Providence, RI 02903	401-277-3505	401-277-6030
SOUTH CAROLINA	South Carolina State Department of Education, Office of Programs for Exceptional Children.	Rutledge Building Room 505 1429 Senate Columbia, SC 29201	803-734-8806	803-734-4824
SOUTH DAKOTA	South Dakota Department of Education & Cultural Affairs, Office of Special Education	700 Governors Drive Pierre, SD 57501-2291	605-773-3315	605-773-6139
TENNESSEE	Tennessee Department of Education, Division of Special Education,	Gateway Plaza 710 James Robertson Parkway 8th Floor Nashville, TN 37243-0380	615-741-2851	615-532-9412
TEXAS	Texas Education Agency, Special Education Unit	W. B. Travis Building Room 5-120 1701 North Congress Avenue Austin, TX 78701-2486	512-463-9414	512-463-9838
UTAH	Utah State Office of Education, Special Education Services Unit	250 East 500 South Salt Lake City, UT 84111-3204	801-538-7711	801-538-7991

74

STATE	DEPARTMENT	ADDRESS	TELEPHONE	FAX
VERMONT	Vermont Department of Education, Division of Special Education	120 State Street State Office Building Montpelier, VT 05602-2501	802-828-5118	802-828-3140
VIRGINIA	Virginia Department of Education, Special Education Department	P.O. Box 2120 Richmond, VA 23216-2120	804-225-2402	804-371-8796
WEST VIRGINIA	West Virginia Department of Education, Office of Special Education	Capitol Complex 1800 Kanawha Boulevard Building 6, Room B-304 Charleston, WV 25305	304-558-2696	304-558-3741
WISCONSIN	Wisconsin Department of Public Instruction, Division Learning Support: Equity & Advocacy	125 South Webster P.O. Box 7841 Madison, WI 53707-7841	608-266-1649	608-267-3746
WYOMING	Wyoming Department of Education, Special Education Unit	Hathaway Building 2nd Floor 2300 Capitol Avenue Cheyenne, WY 82002-0050	307-777-7417	307-777-6234
WASHINGTON	Washington Superintendent of Public Instruction, Special Education Section	Old Capitol Building Olympia, WA 98504-0001	360-753-6733	360-586-0247

APPENDIX 4:
SELECTED PROVISIONS OF SECTION 504
OF THE REHABILITATION ACT OF 1973
(29 U.S.C. SEC. 794)

TITLE 29—LABOR
CHAPTER 16—VOCATIONAL REHABILITATION AND OTHER REHABILITATION SERVICES
SUBCHAPTER V—RIGHTS AND ADVOCACY

* * *

Section 794. Nondiscrimination under Federal grants and programs

(a) Promulgation of rules and regulations

No otherwise qualified individual with a disability in the United States, as defined in section 706(8) of this title, shall, solely by reason of her or his disability, be excluded from the participation in, be denied the benefits of, or be subjected to discrimination under any program or activity receiving Federal financial assistance or under any program or activity conducted by any Executive agency or by the United States Postal Service. The head of each such agency shall promulgate such regulations as may be necessary to carry out the amendments to this section made by the Rehabilitation, Comprehensive Services, and Developmental Disabilities Act of 1978. Copies of any proposed regulation shall be submitted to appropriate authorizing committees of the Congress, and such regulation may take effect no earlier than the thirtieth day after the date on which such regulation is so submitted to such committees.

(b) "Program or activity" defined

For the purposes of this section, the term "program or activity" means all of the operations of—

(1)(A) a department, agency, special purpose district, or other instrumentality of a State or of a local government; or

---

(B) the entity of such State or local government that distributes such assistance and each such department or agency (and each other State or local government entity) to which the assistance is extended, in the case of assistance to a State or local government;

(2)(A) a college, university, or other postsecondary institution, or a public system of higher education; or

(B) a local educational agency (as defined in section 8801 of title 20), system of vocational education, or other school system.

* * *

Section 794a. Remedies and attorney fees

* * *

(b) In any action or proceeding to enforce or charge a violation of a provision of this subchapter, the court, in its discretion, may allow the prevailing party, other than the United States, a reasonable attorney's fee as part of the costs.

* * *

Section 794c. Interagency Disability Coordinating

(a) Establishment

There is hereby established an Interagency Disability Coordinating Council (hereafter in this section referred to as the "Council") composed of the Secretary of Education, the Secretary of Health and Human Services, the Secretary of Labor, the Secretary of Housing and Urban Development, the Secretary of Transportation, the Assistant Secretary of the Interior for Indian Affairs, the Attorney General, the Director of the Office of Personnel Management, the Chairperson of the Equal Employment Opportunity Commission, the Chairperson of the Architectural and Transportation Barriers Compliance Board, and such other officials as may be designated by the President.

(b) Duties

The Council shall—

(1) have the responsibility for developing and implementing agreements, policies, and practices designed to maximize effort, promote efficiency, and eliminate conflict, competition, duplication, and inconsistencies among the operations, functions, and jurisdictions of the various departments, agencies, and branches of the Federal Government responsible for the implementation and enforcement of the provisions of this subchapter, and the regulations prescribed thereunder;

(2) be responsible for developing and implementing agreements, policies, and practices designed to coordinate operations, functions, and jurisdictions of the various departments and agencies of the Federal Government responsible for promoting the full integration into society, independence, and productivity of individuals with disabilities; and

(3) carry out such studies and other activities, subject to the availability of resources, with advice from the National Council on Disability, in order to identify methods for overcoming barriers to integration into society, independence, and productivity of individuals with disabilities.

(c) Report

On or before July 1 of each year, the Interagency Disability Coordinating Council shall prepare and submit to the President and to the Congress a report of the activities of the Council designed to promote and meet the employment needs of individuals with disabilities, together with such recommendations for legislative and administrative changes as the Council concludes are desirable to further promote this section, along with any comments submitted by the National Council on Disability as to the effectiveness of such activities and recommendations in meeting the needs of individuals with disabilities. Nothing in this section shall impair any responsibilities assigned by any Executive order to any Federal department, agency, or instrumentality to act as a lead Federal agency with respect to any provisions of this subchapter.

Section 794d. Electronic and information technology

(a) Requirements for Federal departments and agencies

(1) Accessibility

(A) Development, procurement, maintenance, or use of electronic and information technology

When developing, procuring, maintaining, or using electronic and information technology, each Federal department or agency, including the United States Postal Service, shall ensure, unless an undue burden would be imposed on the department or agency, that the electronic and information technology allows, regardless of the type of medium of the technology—

(i) individuals with disabilities who are Federal employees to have access to and use of information and data that is comparable to the access to and use of the information and data by Federal employees who are not individuals with disabilities; and

(ii) individuals with disabilities who are members of the public seeking information or services from a Federal department or agency to have access to and use of information and data that is comparable to the access to and use of the information and data by such members of the public who are not individuals with disabilities.

(B) Alternative means efforts

When development, procurement, maintenance, or use of electronic and information technology that meets the standards published by the Access Board under paragraph (2) would impose an undue burden, the Federal department or agency shall provide individuals with disabilities covered by paragraph (1) with the information and data involved by an alternative means of access that allows the individual to use the information and data.

* * *

(f) Enforcement

(1) General

(A) Complaints

Effective 6 months after the date of publication by the Access Board of final standards described in subsection (a)(2) of this section, any individual with a disability may file a complaint alleging that a Federal department or agency fails to comply with subsection (a)(1) of this section in providing electronic and information technology.

(B) Application

This subsection shall apply only to electronic and information technology that is procured by a Federal department or agency not less than 6 months after the date of publication by the Access Board of final standards described in subsection (a)(2) of this section.

(2) Administrative complaints

Complaints filed under paragraph (1) shall be filed with the Federal department or agency alleged to be in noncompliance. The Federal department or agency receiving the complaint shall apply the complaint procedures established to implement section 794 of this title for resolving allegations of discrimination in a federally conducted program or activity.

(3) Civil actions

The remedies, procedures, and rights set forth in sections 794a(a)(2) and 794a(b) of this title shall be the remedies, procedures, and rights available to any individual with a disability filing a complaint under paragraph (1).

***

APPENDIX 5:
SELECTED PROVISIONS OF THE INDIVIDUALS WITH DISABILITIES EDUCATION ACT (20 U.S.C. CHAPTER 33)

SUBCHAPTER I— GENERAL PROVISIONS

Section 1400. Congressional Findings and Purpose.

(a) Short Title.

This chapter may be cited as the "Individuals with Disabilities Education Act."

(b) omitted.

(c) Findings.

The Congress finds the following:

(1) Disability is a natural part of the human experience and in no way diminishes the right of individuals to participate in or contribute to society. Improving educational results for children with disabilities is an essential element of our national policy of ensuring equality of opportunity, full participation, independent living, and economic self-sufficiency for individuals with disabilities.

(2) Before the date of the enactment of the Education for All Handicapped Children Act of 1975 (Public Law 94-142)—

(A) the special educational needs of children with disabilities were not being fully met;

(B) more than one-half of the children with disabilities in the United States did not receive appropriate educational services that would enable such children to have full equality of opportunity;

(C) 1,000,000 of the children with disabilities in the United States were excluded entirely from the public school system and did not go through the educational process with their peers;

(D) there were many children with disabilities throughout the United States participating in regular school programs whose disabilities prevented such children from having a successful educational experience because their disabilities were undetected; and

(E) because of the lack of adequate services within the public school system, families were often forced to find services outside the public school system, often at great distance from their residence and at their own expense.

(3) Since the enactment and implementation of the Education for All Handicapped Children Act of 1975, this Act has been successful in ensuring children with disabilities and the families of such children access to a free appropriate public education and in improving educational results for children with disabilities.

* * *

(d) Purposes.

The purposes of this title are—

(1)(A) to ensure that all children with disabilities have available to them a free appropriate public education that emphasizes special education and related services designed to meet their unique needs and prepare them for employment and independent living;

(B) to ensure that the rights of children with disabilities and parents of such children are protected; and

(C) to assist States, localities, educational service agencies, and Federal agencies to provide for the education of all children with disabilities;

(2) to assist States in the implementation of a statewide, comprehensive, coordinated, multidisciplinary, interagency system of early intervention services for infants and toddlers with disabilities and their families;

(3) to ensure that educators and parents have the necessary tools to improve educational results for children with disabilities by supporting systemic-change activities; coordinated research and personnel preparation; coordinated technical assistance, dissemination, and support; and technology development and media services; and

(4) to assess, and ensure the effectiveness of, efforts to educate children with disabilities.

* * *

Section 1402. Office of Special Education Programs.

(a) Establishment.

There shall be, within the Office of Special Education and Rehabilitative Services in the Department of Education, an Office of Special Education Programs, which shall be the principal agency in such Department for administering and carrying out this Act and other programs and activities concerning the education of children with disabilities.

(b) Director.

The Office established under subsection (a) shall be headed by a Director who shall be selected by the Secretary and shall report directly to the Assistant Secretary for Special Education and Rehabilitative Services.

(c) Voluntary and Uncompensated Services.

Notwithstanding section 1342 of title 31, United States Code, the Secretary is authorized to accept voluntary and uncompensated services in furtherance of the purposes of this Act.

Section 1403. Abrogation of State Sovereign Immunity.

(a) In General.

A State shall not be immune under the eleventh amendment to the Constitution of the United States from suit in Federal court for a violation of this Act.

(b) Remedies.

In a suit against a State for a violation of this Act, remedies (including remedies both at law and in equity) are available for such a violation to the same extent as those remedies are available for such a violation in the suit against any public entity other than a State.

(c) Effective Date.

Subsections (a) and (b) apply with respect to violations that occur in whole or part after the date of the enactment of the Education of the Handicapped Act Amendments of 1990.

* * *

SUBCHAPTER II— ASSISTANCE FOR EDUCATION OF ALL CHILDREN WITH DISABILITIES

Section 1412. State eligibility.

(1) Free Appropriate Public Education.

(A) In General. A free appropriate public education is available to all children with disabilities residing in the State between the ages of 3 and 21, inclusive, including children with disabilities who have been suspended or expelled from school.

(B) Limitation. The obligation to make a free appropriate public education available to all children with disabilities does not apply with respect to children:

(i) aged 3 through 5 and 18 through 21 in a State to the extent that its application to those children would be inconsistent with State law or practice, or the order of any court, respecting the provision of public education to children in those age ranges; and

(ii) aged 18 through 21 to the extent that State law does not require that special education and related services under this part be provided to children with disabilities who, in the educational placement prior to their incarceration in an adult correctional facility:

(I) were not actually identified as being a child with a disability under Section 1402(3) of this Act; or

(II) did not have an individualized education program under this part.

(2) Full Educational Opportunity Goal. The State has established a goal of providing full educational opportunity to all children with disabilities and a detailed timetable for accomplishing that goal.

(3) Child Find.

(A) In General. All children with disabilities residing in the State, including children with disabilities attending private schools, regardless of the severity of their disabilities, and who are in need of special education and related services, are identified, located, and evaluated and a practical method is developed and implemented to determine which children with disabilities are currently receiving needed special education and related services.

(B) Construction. Nothing in this Act requires that children be classified by their disability so long as each child who has a disability listed in Section 1402 and who, by reason of that disability, needs special education and related services is regarded as a child with a disability under this part.

(4) Individualized Education Program. An individualized education program, or an individualized family service plan that meets the requirements of Section 1436(d), is developed, reviewed, and revised for each child with a disability in accordance with Section 1414(d).

(5) Least Restrictive Environment.

(A) In General. To the maximum extent appropriate, children with disabilities, including children in public or private institutions or other care facilities, are educated with children who are not disabled, and special classes, separate schooling, or other removal of children with disabilities from the regular educational environment occurs only when the nature or severity of the disability of a child is such that education in regular classes with the use of supplementary aids and services cannot be achieved satisfactorily.

(B) Additional Requirement.

(i) In General. If the State uses a funding mechanism by which the State distributes State funds on the basis of the type of setting in which a child is served, the funding mechanism does not result in placements that violate the requirements of subparagraph (A).

(ii) Assurance. If the State does not have policies and procedures to ensure compliance with clause (i), the State shall provide the Secretary an assurance that it will revise the funding mechanism as soon as feasible to ensure that such mechanism does not result in such placements.

(6) Procedural Safeguards.

(A) In General. Children with disabilities and their parents are afforded the procedural safeguards required by Section 1415.

(B) Additional Procedural Safeguards. Procedures to ensure that testing and evaluation materials and procedures utilized for the purposes of evaluation and placement of children with disabilities will be selected and administered so as not to be racially or culturally discriminatory. Such materials or procedures shall be provided and administered in the child's native language or mode of communication, unless it clearly is not feasible to do so, and no single procedure shall be the sole criterion for determining an appropriate educational program for a child.

(7) Evaluation. Children with disabilities are evaluated in accordance with subsections (a) through (c) of Section 1414.

(8) Confidentiality. Agencies in the State comply with Section 1417(c) (relating to the confidentiality of records and information).

(9) Transition From subchapter III to Preschool Programs. Children participating in early-intervention programs assisted under subchapter III, and who will participate in preschool programs assisted under this subchapter, experience a smooth and effective transition to those preschool programs in a manner consistent with Section 1437(a)(8). By the third birthday of such a child, an individualized education program or, if consistent with sections 1414(d)(2)(B) and 1436(d), an individualized family service plan, has been developed and is being implemented for the child. The local educational agency will participate in transition planning conferences arranged by the designated lead agency under Section 1437(a)(8).

(10) Children in Private Schools.

    (A) Children Enrolled in Private Schools by Their Parents.

        (i) In General. To the extent consistent with the number and location of children with disabilities in the State who are enrolled by their parents in private elementary and secondary schools, provision is made for the participation of those children in the program assisted or carried out under this part by providing for such children education and related services in accordance with the following requirements, unless the Secretary has arranged for services to those children under subsection (f):

            (I) Amounts expended for the provision of those services by a local educational agency shall be equal to a proportionate amount of Federal funds made available under this part.

            (II) Such services may be provided to children with disabilities on the premises of private, including parochial, schools, to the extent consistent with law.

        (ii) Child-find Requirement. The requirements of paragraph (3) of this subsection (relating to child find) shall apply with respect to children with disabilities in the State who are enrolled in private, including parochial, elementary and secondary schools.

    (B) Children Placed in, or Referred to, Private Schools by Public Agencies.

        (i) In General. Children with disabilities in private schools and facilities are provided special education and related services, in accordance with an individualized education program, at no cost to their parents, if such children are placed in, or referred to, such schools or facilities by the State or appropriate local educational agency as the means of carrying out the requirements of this part or any other applicable law requiring the provision of special education and related services to all children with disabilities within such State.

(ii) Standards. In all cases described in clause (i), the State educational agency shall determine whether such schools and facilities meet standards that apply to State and local educational agencies and that children so served have all the rights they would have if served by such agencies.

(C) Payment for Education of Children Enrolled in Private Schools without Consent of or Referral by the Public Agency.

(i) In General. Subject to subparagraph (A), this part does not require a local educational agency to pay for the cost of education, including special education and related services, of a child with a disability at a private school or facility if that agency made a free appropriate public education available to the child and the parents elected to place the child in such private school or facility.

(ii) Reimbursement for Private School Placement. If the parents of a child with a disability, who previously received special education and related services under the authority of a public agency, enroll the child in a private elementary or secondary school without the consent of or referral by the public agency, a court or a hearing officer may require the agency to reimburse the parents for the cost of that enrollment if the court or hearing officer finds that the agency had not made a free appropriate public education available to the child in a timely manner prior to that enrollment.

(iii) Limitation On Reimbursement. The cost of reimbursement described in clause (ii) may be reduced or denied—

(I) if—

(aa) at the most recent IEP meeting that the parents attended prior to removal of the child from the public school, the parents did not inform the IEP Team that they were rejecting the placement proposed by the public agency to provide a free appropriate public education to their child, including stating their concerns and their intent to enroll their child in a private school at public expense;

(bb) 10 business days (including any holidays that occur on a business day) prior to the removal of the child from the public school, the parents did not give written notice to the public agency of the information described in division (aa);

(II) if, prior to the parents' removal of the child from the public school, the public agency informed the parents, through the notice requirements described in Section 1415(b)(7), of its intent to evaluate the child (including a statement of the purpose of the evaluation that was appropriate and reasonable), but the parents did not make the child available for such evaluation; or

(III) upon a judicial finding of unreasonableness with respect to actions taken by the parents.

(iv) Exception. Notwithstanding the notice requirement in clause (iii)(I), the cost of reimbursement may not be reduced or denied for failure to provide such notice if—

(I) the parent is illiterate and cannot write in English;

(II) compliance with clause (iii)(I) would likely result in physical or serious emotional harm to the child;

(III) the school prevented the parent from providing such notice; or

(IV) the parents had not received notice, pursuant to Section 1415, of the notice requirement in clause (iii)(I).

(11) State Educational Agency Responsible for General Supervision.

(A) In General. The State educational agency is responsible for ensuring that—

(i) the requirements of this part are met; and

(ii) all educational programs for children with disabilities in the State, including all such programs administered by any other State or local agency—

(I) are under the general supervision of individuals in the State who are responsible for educational programs for children with disabilities; and

(II) meet the educational standards of the State educational agency.

(B) Limitation. Subparagraph (A) shall not limit the responsibility of agencies in the State other than the State educational agency to provide, or pay for some or all of the costs of, a free appropriate public education for any child with a disability in the State.

* * *

(15) Personnel Standards.

(A) In General. The State educational agency has established and maintains standards to ensure that personnel necessary to carry out this part are appropriately and adequately prepared and trained.

(C) Policy. In implementing this paragraph, a State may adopt a policy that includes a requirement that local educational agencies in the State make an ongoing good-faith effort to recruit and hire appropriately and adequately trained personnel to provide special education and related services to children with disabilities, including, in a geographic area of the State where there is a shortage of such personnel, the most qualified individuals available who are making satisfactory progress toward completing applicable course work necessary to meet the standards described in subparagraph (B)(i), consistent with State law, and the steps described in subparagraph (B)(ii) within three years.

* * *

(17) Participation in Assessments.

(A) In General. Children with disabilities are included in general State and district-wide assessment programs, with appropriate accommodations, where necessary. As appropriate, the State or local educational agency—

(i) develops guidelines for the participation of children with disabilities in alternate assessments for those children who cannot participate in State and district-wide assessment programs; and

(ii) develops and, beginning not later than July 1, 2000, conducts those alternate assessments.

* * *

(19) Maintenance of State Financial Support.

(A) In General. The State does not reduce the amount of State financial support for special education and related services for children with disabilities, or otherwise made available because of the excess costs of educating those children, below the amount of that support for the preceding fiscal year.

(B) Reduction of Funds for Failure to Maintain Support. The Secretary shall reduce the allocation of funds under Section 1411 for any fiscal year following the fiscal year in which the State fails to comply with the requirement of subparagraph (A) by the same amount by which the State fails to meet the requirement.

(C) Waivers for Exceptional or Uncontrollable Circumstances. The Secretary may waive the requirement of subparagraph (A) for a State, for one fiscal year at a time, if the Secretary determines that—

(i) granting a waiver would be equitable due to exceptional or uncontrollable circumstances such as a natural disaster or a precipitous and unforeseen decline in the financial resources of the State; or

(ii) the State meets the standard in paragraph (18)(C) of this section for a waiver of the requirement to supplement, and not to supplant, funds received under this part.

(20) Public Participation. Prior to the adoption of any policies and procedures needed to comply with this section (including any amendments to such policies and procedures), the State ensures that there are public hearings, adequate notice of the hearings, and an opportunity for comment available to the general public, including individuals with disabilities and parents of children with disabilities.

(21) State Advisory Panel.

(A) In General. The State has established and maintains an advisory panel for the purpose of providing policy guidance with respect to special education and related services for children with disabilities in the State.

(B) Membership. Such advisory panel shall consist of members appointed by the Governor, or any other official authorized under State law to make such appointments, that is representative of the State population and that is composed of individuals involved in, or concerned with, the education of children with disabilities, including—

(i) parents of children with disabilities;

(ii) individuals with disabilities;

(iii) teachers;

(iv) representatives of institutions of higher education that prepare special education and related services personnel;

(v) State and local education officials;

(vi) administrators of programs for children with disabilities;

(vii) representatives of other State agencies involved in the financing or delivery of related services to children with disabilities;

(viii) representatives of private schools and public charter schools;

(ix) at least one representative of a vocational, community, or business organization concerned with the provision of transition services to children with disabilities; and @P2 = (x) representatives from the State juvenile and adult corrections agencies.

(C) Special Rule. A majority of the members of the panel shall be individuals with disabilities or parents of children with disabilities.

(D) Duties. The advisory panel shall—

(i) advise the State educational agency of unmet needs within the State in the education of children with disabilities;

(ii) comment publicly on any rules or regulations proposed by the State regarding the education of children with disabilities;

(iii) advise the State educational agency in developing evaluations and reporting on data to the Secretary under Section 1418;

(iv) advise the State educational agency in developing corrective action plans to address findings identified in Federal monitoring reports under this part; and

(v) advise the State educational agency in developing and implementing policies relating to the coordination of services for children with disabilities.

* * *

Section 1413. Local Educational Agency Eligibility.

(a) In General.

A local educational agency is eligible for assistance under this part for a fiscal year if such agency demonstrates to the satisfaction of the State educational agency that it meets each of the following conditions:

(1) Consistency with State Policies. The local educational agency, in providing for the education of children with disabilities within its jurisdiction, has in effect policies, procedures, and programs that are consistent with the State policies and procedures established under Section 1412.

(2) Use of Amounts.

(A) In General. Amounts provided to the local educational agency under this part shall be expended in accordance with the applicable provisions of this part and—

(i) shall be used only to pay the excess costs of providing special education and related services to children with disabilities;

(ii) shall be used to supplement State, local, and other Federal funds and not to supplant such funds; and

(iii) shall not be used, except as provided in subparagraphs (B) and (C), to reduce the level of expenditures for the education of children with disabilities made by the local educational agency from local funds below the level of those expenditures for the preceding fiscal year.

* * *

(6) Additional Requirements.

(A) Parental Involvement. In carrying out the requirements of this subsection, a local educational agency shall ensure that the parents of children with disabilities are involved in the design, evaluation, and, where appropriate, implementation of school-based improvement plans in accordance with this subsection.

(j) Disciplinary Information.

The State may require that a local educational agency include in the records of a child with a disability a statement of any current or previous disciplinary action that has been taken against the child and transmit such statement to the same extent that such disciplinary information is included in, and transmitted with, the student records of nondisabled children. The statement may include a description of any behavior engaged in by the child that required disciplinary action, a description of the disciplinary action taken, and any other information that is relevant to the safety of the child and other individuals involved with the child. If the State adopts such a policy, and the child transfers from one school to another, the transmission of any of the child's records must include both the child's current individualized education program and any such statement of current or previous disciplinary action that has been taken against the child.

Section 1414. Evaluations, Eligibility Determinations, Individualized Education Programs, and Educational Placements.

(a) Evaluations and Re-evaluations.

(1) Initial Evaluations.

(A) In General. A State educational agency, other State agency, or local educational agency shall conduct a full and individual initial evaluation, in accordance with this paragraph and subsection (b), before the initial provision of special education and related services to a child with a disability under this part.

(B) Procedures. Such initial evaluation shall consist of procedures—

(i) to determine whether a child is a child with a disability (as defined in Section 1402(3)); and

(ii) to determine the educational needs of such child.

(C) Parental Consent.

(i) In General. The agency proposing to conduct an initial evaluation to determine if the child qualifies as a child with a disability as defined in Section 1402(3)(A) or 602(3)(B) shall obtain an informed consent from the parent of such child before the evaluation is conducted. Parental consent for evaluation shall not be construed as consent for placement for receipt of special education and related services.

(ii) Refusal. If the parents of such child refuse consent for the evaluation, the agency may continue to pursue an evaluation by utilizing the mediation and due process procedures under Section 1415, except to the extent inconsistent with State law relating to parental consent.

(2) Re-evaluations. A local educational agency shall ensure that a reevaluation of each child with a disability is conducted—

(A) if conditions warrant a reevaluation or if the child's parent or teacher requests a reevaluation, but at least once every 3 years; and

(B) in accordance with subsections (b) and (c).

(b) Evaluation Procedures.

(1) Notice. The local educational agency shall provide notice to the parents of a child with a disability, in accordance with subsections (b)(3), (b)(4), and (c) of Section 1415, that describes any evaluation procedures such agency proposes to conduct.

(2) Conduct of Evaluation. In conducting the evaluation, the local educational agency shall—

(A) use a variety of assessment tools and strategies to gather relevant functional and developmental information, including information provided by the parent, that may assist in determining whether the child is a child with a disability and the content of the child's individualized education program, including information related to enabling the child to be involved in and progress in the general curriculum or, for preschool children, to participate in appropriate activities;

(B) not use any single procedure as the sole criterion for determining whether a child is a child with a disability or determining an appropriate educational program for the child; and

(C) use technically sound instruments that may assess the relative contribution of cognitive and behavioral factors, in addition to physical or developmental factors.

(3) Additional Requirements. Each local educational agency shall ensure that—

(A) tests and other evaluation materials used to assess a child under this section—

(i) are selected and administered so as not to be discriminatory on a racial or cultural basis; and

(ii) are provided and administered in the child's native language or other mode of communication, unless it is clearly not feasible to do so; and

(B) any standardized tests that are given to the child—

(i) have been validated for the specific purpose for which they are used;

(ii) are administered by trained and knowledgeable personnel; and

(iii) are administered in accordance with any instructions provided by the producer of such tests;

(C) the child is assessed in all areas of suspected disability; and

(D) assessment tools and strategies that provide relevant information that directly assists persons in determining the educational needs of the child are provided.

(4) Determination of Eligibility. Upon completion of administration of tests and other evaluation materials—

(A) the determination of whether the child is a child with a disability as defined in Section 1402(3) shall be made by a team of qualified professionals and the parent of the child in accordance with paragraph (5); and

(B) a copy of the evaluation report and the documentation of determination of eligibility will be given to the parent.

(5) Special Rule for Eligibility Determination. In making a determination of eligibility under paragraph (4)(A), a child shall not be determined to be a child with a disability if the determinant factor for such

determination is lack of instruction in reading or math or limited English proficiency.

(c) Additional Requirements for Evaluation and Re-evaluations.

(1) Review of Existing Evaluation Data. As part of an initial evaluation (if appropriate) and as part of any reevaluation under this section, the IEP Team described in subsection (d)(1)(B) and other qualified professionals, as appropriate, shall—

(A) review existing evaluation data on the child, including evaluations and information provided by the parents of the child, current classroom-based assessments and observations, and teacher and related services providers observation; and

(B) on the basis of that review, and input from the child's parents, identify what additional data, if any, are needed to determine—

(i) whether the child has a particular category of disability, as described in Section 1402(3), or, in case of a reevaluation of a child, whether the child continues to have such a disability;

(ii) the present levels of performance and educational needs of the child;

(iii) whether the child needs special education and related services, or in the case of a reevaluation of a child, whether the child continues to need special education and related services; and

(iv) whether any additions or modifications to the special education and related services are needed to enable the child to meet the measurable annual goals set out in the individualized education program of the child and to participate, as appropriate, in the general curriculum.

(2) Source of Data. The local educational agency shall administer such tests and other evaluation materials as may be needed to produce the data identified by the IEP Team under paragraph (1)(B).

(3) Parental Consent. Each local educational agency shall obtain informed parental consent, in accordance with subsection (a)(1)(C), prior to conducting any reevaluation of a child with a disability, except that such informed parent consent need not be obtained if the local educational agency can demonstrate that it had taken reasonable measures to obtain such consent and the child's parent has failed to respond.

(4) Requirements If Additional Data Are Not Needed. If the IEP Team and other qualified professionals, as appropriate, determine that no addi-

tional data are needed to determine whether the child continues to be a child with a disability, the local educational agency—

(A) shall notify the child's parents of—

(i) that determination and the reasons for it; and

(ii) the right of such parents to request an assessment to determine whether the child continues to be a child with a disability; and

(B) shall not be required to conduct such an assessment unless requested to by the child's parents.

(5) Evaluations Before Change in Eligibility. A local educational agency shall evaluate a child with a disability in accordance with this section before determining that the child is no longer a child with a disability.

(d) Individualized Education Programs.

(1) Definitions. As used in this title:

(A) Individualized Education Program. The term `individualized education program' or `IEP' means a written statement for each cnild with a disability that is developed, reviewed, and revised in accordance with this section and that includes—

(i) a statement of the child's present levels of educational performance, including—

(I) how the child's disability affects the child's involvement and progress in the general curriculum; or

(II) for preschool children, as appropriate, how the disability affects the child's participation in appropriate activities;

(ii) a statement of measurable annual goals, including benchmarks or short-term objectives, related to—

(I) meeting the child's needs that result from the child's disability to enable the child to be involved in and progress in the general curriculum; and

(II) meeting each of the child's other educational needs that result from the child's disability; (iii) a statement of the special education and related services and supplementary aids and services to be provided to the child, or on behalf of the child, and a statement of the program modifications or supports for school personnel that will be provided for the child—

(I) to advance appropriately toward attaining the annual goals;

(II) to be involved and progress in the general curriculum in accordance with clause (i) and to participate in extracurricular and other nonacademic activities; and

(III) to be educated and participate with other children with disabilities and nondisabled children in the activities described in this paragraph;

(iv) an explanation of the extent, if any, to which the child will not participate with nondisabled children in the regular class and in the activities described in clause (iii);

(v)(I) a statement of any individual modifications in the administration of State or districtwide assessments of student achievement that are needed in order for the child to participate in such assessment; and

(II) if the IEP Team determines that the child will not participate in a particular State or districtwide assessment of student achievement (or part of such an assessment), a statement of—

(aa) why that assessment is not appropriate for the child; and

(bb) how the child will be assessed;

(vi) the projected date for the beginning of the services and modifications described in clause (iii), and the anticipated frequency, location, and duration of those services and modifications;

(vii)(I) beginning at age 14, and updated annually, a statement of the transition service needs of the child under the applicable components of the child's IEP that focuses on the child's courses of study (such as participation in advanced-placement courses or a vocational education program);

(II) beginning at age 16 (or younger, if determined appropriate by the IEP Team), a statement of needed transition services for the child, including, when appropriate, a statement of the interagency responsibilities or any needed linkages; and

(III) beginning at least one year before the child reaches the age of majority under State law, a statement that the child has been informed of his or her rights under this title, if any, that will transfer to the child on reaching the age of majority under Section 1415(m); and

(viii) a statement of—

(I) how the child's progress toward the annual goals described in clause (ii) will be measured; and

(II) how the child's parents will be regularly informed (by such means as periodic report cards), at least as often as parents are informed of their nondisabled children's progress, of—

(aa) their child's progress toward the annual goals described in clause (ii); and

(bb) the extent to which that progress is sufficient to enable the child to achieve the goals by the end of the year.

(B) Individualized Education Program Team. The term 'individualized education program team' or 'IEP Team' means a group of individuals composed of—

(i) the parents of a child with a disability;

(ii) at least one regular education teacher of such child (if the child is, or may be, participating in the regular education environment);

(iii) at least one special education teacher, or where appropriate, at least one special education provider of such child;

(iv) a representative of the local educational agency who—

(I) is qualified to provide, or supervise the provision of, specially designed instruction to meet the unique needs of children with disabilities;

(II) is knowledgeable about the general curriculum; and

(III) is knowledgeable about the availability of resources of the local educational agency;

(v) an individual who can interpret the instructional implications of evaluation results, who may be a member of the team described in clauses (ii) through (vi);

(vi) at the discretion of the parent or the agency, other individuals who have knowledge or special expertise regarding the child, including related services personnel as appropriate; and

(vii) whenever appropriate, the child with a disability.

(2) Requirement That Program Be in Effect.

(A) In General. At the beginning of each school year, each local educational agency, State educational agency, or other State agency, as the case may be, shall have in effect, for each child with a disability in its jurisdiction, an individualized education program, as defined in paragraph (1)(A).

(B) Program for Child Aged 3 Through 5. In the case of a child with a disability aged 3 through 5 (or, at the discretion of the State educational agency, a 2 year-old child with a disability who will turn age 3 during the school year), an individualized family service plan that contains the material described in Section 1436, and that is developed in accordance with this section, may serve as the IEP of the child if using that plan as the IEP is—

(i) consistent with State policy; and

(ii) agreed to by the agency and the child's parents.

(3) Development of IEP.

(A) In General. In developing each child's IEP, the IEP Team, subject to subparagraph (C), shall consider—

(i) the strengths of the child and the concerns of the parents for enhancing the education of their child; and

(ii) the results of the initial evaluation or most recent evaluation of the child.

(B) Consideration of Special Factors. The IEP Team shall—

(i) in the case of a child whose behavior impedes his or her learning or that of others, consider, when appropriate, strategies, including positive behavioral interventions, strategies, and supports to address that behavior;

(ii) in the case of a child with limited English proficiency, consider the language needs of the child as such needs relate to the child's IEP;

(iii) in the case of a child who is blind or visually impaired, provide for instruction in Braille and the use of Braille unless the IEP Team determines, after an evaluation of the child's reading and writing skills, needs, and appropriate reading and writing media (including an evaluation of the child's future needs for instruction in Braille or the use of Braille), that instruction in Braille or the use of Braille is not appropriate for the child;

(iv) consider the communication needs of the child, and in the case of a child who is deaf or hard of hearing, consider the child's language and communication needs, opportunities for direct communications with peers and professional personnel in the child's language and communication mode, academic level, and full range of needs, including opportunities for direct instruction in the child's language and communication mode; and

(v) consider whether the child requires assistive technology devices and services.

(C) Requirement with Respect to Regular Education Teacher. The regular education teacher of the child, as a member of the IEP Team, shall, to the extent appropriate, participate in the development of the IEP of the child, including the determination of appropriate positive behavioral interventions and strategies and the determination of supplementary aids and services, program modifications, and support for school personnel consistent with paragraph (1)(A)(iii).

(4) Review and Revision of IEP.

(A) In General. The local educational agency shall ensure that, subject to subparagraph (B), the IEP Team—

(i) reviews the child's IEP periodically, but not less than annually to determine whether the annual goals for the child are being achieved; and

(ii) revises the IEP as appropriate to address—

(I) any lack of expected progress toward the annual goals and in the general curriculum, where appropriate;

(II) the results of any reevaluation conducted under this section;

(III) information about the child provided to, or by, the parents, as described in subsection (c)(1)(B);

(IV) the child's anticipated needs; or (V) other matters.

(B) Requirement with Respect to Regular Education Teacher. The regular education teacher of the child, as a member of the IEP Team, shall, to the extent appropriate, participate in the review and revision of the IEP of the child.

(5) Failure to Meet Transition Objectives. If a participating agency, other than the local educational agency, fails to provide the transition services described in the IEP in accordance with paragraph (1)(A)(vii), the local educational agency shall reconvene the IEP Team to identify alternative strategies to meet the transition objectives for the child set out in that program.

* * *

(f) Educational Placements.

Each local educational agency or State educational agency shall ensure that the parents of each child with a disability are members of any group that makes decisions on the educational placement of their child.

Section 1415. Procedural Safeguards.

(a) Establishment of Procedures.

Any State educational agency, State agency, or local educational agency that receives assistance under this part shall establish and maintain procedures in accordance with this section to ensure that children with disabilities and their parents are guaranteed procedural safeguards with respect to the provision of free appropriate public education by such agencies.

(b) Types of Procedures.

The procedures required by this section shall include—

(1) an opportunity for the parents of a child with a disability to examine all records relating to such child and to participate in meetings with respect to the identification, evaluation, and educational placement of the child, and the provision of a free appropriate public education to such child, and to obtain an independent educational evaluation of the child;

(2) procedures to protect the rights of the child whenever the parents of the child are not known, the agency cannot, after reasonable efforts, locate the parents, or the child is a ward of the State, including the assignment of an individual (who shall not be an employee of the State educational agency, the local educational agency, or any other agency that is involved in the education or care of the child) to act as a surrogate for the parents;

(3) written prior notice to the parents of the child whenever such agency—

(A) proposes to initiate or change; or

(B) refuses to initiate or change; the identification, evaluation, or educational placement of the child, in accordance with subsection (c), or the provision of a free appropriate public education to the child;

(4) procedures designed to ensure that the notice required by paragraph (3) is in the native language of the parents, unless it clearly is not feasible to do so;

(5) an opportunity for mediation in accordance with subsection (e);

(6) an opportunity to present complaints with respect to any matter relating to the identification, evaluation, or educational placement

of the child, or the provision of a free appropriate public education to such child;

(7) procedures that require the parent of a child with a disability, or the attorney representing the child, to provide notice (which shall remain confidential)—

(A) to the State educational agency or local educational agency, as the case may be, in the complaint filed under paragraph (6); and

(B) that shall include—

(i) the name of the child, the address of the residence of the child, and the name of the school the child is attending;

(ii) a description of the nature of the problem of the child relating to such proposed initiation or change, including facts relating to such problem; and

(iii) a proposed resolution of the problem to the extent known and available to the parents at the time; and

(8) procedures that require the State educational agency to develop a model form to as*sist parents in filing a complaint in accordance with paragraph (7).

(c) Content of Prior Written Notice.

The notice required by subsection (b)(3) shall include—

(1) a description of the action proposed or refused by the agency;

(2) an explanation of why the agency proposes or refuses to take the action;

(3) a description of any other options that the agency considered and the reasons why those options were rejected;

(4) a description of each evaluation procedure, test, record, or report the agency used as a basis for the proposed or refused action;

(5) a description of any other factors that are relevant to the agency's proposal or refusal;

(6) a statement that the parents of a child with a disability have protection under the procedural safeguards of this part and, if this notice is not an initial referral for evaluation, the means by which a copy of a description of the procedural safeguards can be obtained; and

(7) sources for parents to contact to obtain assistance in understanding the provisions of this part.

(d) Procedural Safeguards Notice.

(1) In General. A copy of the procedural safeguards available to the parents of a child with a disability shall be given to the parents, at a minimum—

(A) upon initial referral for evaluation;

(B) upon each notification of an individualized education program meeting and upon reevaluation of the child; and

(C) upon registration of a complaint under subsection (b)(6).

(2) Contents. The procedural safeguards notice shall include a full explanation of the procedural safeguards, written in the native language of the parents, unless it clearly is not feasible to do so, and written in an easily understandable manner, available under this section and under regulations promulgated by the Secretary relating to—

(A) independent educational evaluation;

(B) prior written notice;

(C) parental consent;

(D) access to educational records;

(E) opportunity to present complaints;

(F) the child's placement during pendency of due process proceedings;

(G) procedures for students who are subject to placement in an interim alternative educational setting;

(H) requirements for unilateral placement by parents of children in private schools at public expense;

(I) mediation;

(J) due process hearings, including requirements for disclosure of evaluation results and recommendations;

(K) State-level appeals (if applicable in that State);

(L) civil actions; and

(M) attorneys' fees.

(e) Mediation.

(1) In General. Any State educational agency or local educational agency that receives assistance under this part shall ensure that procedures are established and implemented to allow parties to disputes involving any matter described in subsection (b)(6) to resolve such

disputes through a mediation process which, at a minimum, shall be available whenever a hearing is requested under subsection (f) or (k).

(2) Requirements. Such procedures shall meet the following requirements:

(A) The procedures shall ensure that the mediation process—

(i) is voluntary on the part of the parties;

(ii) is not used to deny or delay a parent's right to a due process hearing under subsection (f), or to deny any other rights afforded under this part; and

(iii) is conducted by a qualified and impartial mediator who is trained in effective mediation techniques.

(B) A local educational agency or a State agency may establish procedures to require parents who choose not to use the mediation process to meet, at a time and location convenient to the parents, with a disinterested party who is under contract with—

(i) a parent training and information center or community parent resource center in the State established under Section 1482 or 1483; or

(ii) an appropriate alternative dispute resolution entity;

to encourage the use, and explain the benefits, of the mediation process to the parents.

(C) The State shall maintain a list of individuals who are qualified mediators and knowledgeable in laws and regulations relating to the provision of special education and related services.

(D) The State shall bear the cost of the mediation process, including the costs of meetings described in subparagraph (B).

(E) Each session in the mediation process shall be scheduled in a timely manner and shall be held in a location that is convenient to the parties to the dispute.

(F) An agreement reached by the parties to the dispute in the mediation process shall be set forth in a written mediation agreement.

(G) Discussions that occur during the mediation process shall be confidential and may not be used as evidence in any subsequent due process hearings or civil proceedings and the parties to the mediation process may be required to sign a confidentiality pledge prior to the commencement of such process.

(f) Impartial Due Process Hearing.

(1) In General. Whenever a complaint has been received under subsection (b)(6) or (k) of this section, the parents involved in such complaint shall have an opportunity for an impartial due process hearing, which shall be conducted by the State educational agency or by the local educational agency, as determined by State law or by the State educational agency.

(2) Disclosure of Evaluations and Recommendations.

(A) In General. At least 5 business days prior to a hearing conducted pursuant to paragraph (1), each party shall disclose to all other parties all evaluations completed by that date and recommendations based on the offering party's evaluations that the party intends to use at the hearing.

(B) Failure to Disclose. A hearing officer may bar any party that fails to comply with subparagraph (A) from introducing the relevant evaluation or recommendation at the hearing without the consent of the other party.

(3) Limitation on Conduct of Hearing. A hearing conducted pursuant to paragraph (1) may not be conducted by an employee of the State educational agency or the local educational agency involved in the education or care of the child.

(g) Appeal.

If the hearing required by subsection (f) is conducted by a local educational agency, any party aggrieved by the findings and decision rendered in such a hearing may appeal such findings and decision to the State educational agency. Such agency shall conduct an impartial review of such decision. The officer conducting such review shall make an independent decision upon completion of such review.

(h) Safeguards.

Any party to a hearing conducted pursuant to subsection (f) or (k), or an appeal conducted pursuant to subsection (g), shall be accorded—

(1) the right to be accompanied and advised by counsel and by individuals with special knowledge or training with respect to the problems of children with disabilities;

(2) the right to present evidence and confront, cross-examine, and compel the attendance of witnesses;

(3) the right to a written, or, at the option of the parents, electronic verbatim record of such hearing; and

(4) the right to written, or, at the option of the parents, electronic findings of fact and decisions (which findings and decisions shall be made available to the public consistent with the requirements of Section 1417(c) (relating to the confidentiality of data, information, and records) and shall also be transmitted to the advisory panel established pursuant to Section 1412(a)(21)).

(i) Administrative Procedures.

(1) In General.

(A) Decision Made in Hearing. A decision made in a hearing conducted pursuant to subsection (f) or (k) shall be final, except that any party involved in such hearing may appeal such decision under the provisions of subsection (g) and paragraph (2) of this subsection.

(B) Decision Made at Appeal. A decision made under subsection (g) shall be final, except that any party may bring an action under paragraph (2) of this subsection.

(2) Right to Bring Civil Action.

(A) In General. Any party aggrieved by the findings and decision made under subsection (f) or (k) who does not have the right to an appeal under subsection (g), and any party aggrieved by the findings and decision under this subsection, shall have the right to bring a civil action with respect to the complaint presented pursuant to this section, which action may be brought in any State court of competent jurisdiction or in a district court of the United States without regard to the amount in controversy.

(B) Additional Requirements. In any action brought under this paragraph, the court—

(i) shall receive the records of the administrative proceedings;

(ii) shall hear additional evidence at the request of a party; and

(iii) basing its decision on the preponderance of the evidence, shall grant such relief as the court determines is appropriate.

(3) Jurisdiction of District Courts; Attorneys' Fees.

(A) In General. The district courts of the United States shall have jurisdiction of actions brought under this section without regard to the amount in controversy.

(B) Award of Attorneys' Fees. In any action or proceeding brought under this section, the court, in its discretion, may award reasonable attorneys' fees as part of the costs to the parents of a child with a disability who is the prevailing party.

(C) Determination of Amount of Attorneys' Fees. Fees awarded under this paragraph shall be based on rates prevailing in the community in which the action or proceeding arose for the kind and quality of services furnished. No bonus or multiplier may be used in calculating the fees awarded under this subsection.

(D) Prohibition of Attorneys' Fees and Related Costs for Certain Services.

(i) Attorneys' fees may not be awarded and related costs may not be reimbursed in any action or proceeding under this section for services performed subsequent to the time of a written offer of settlement to a parent if—

(I) the offer is made within the time prescribed by Rule 68 of the Federal Rules of Civil Procedure or, in the case of an administrative proceeding, at any time more than 10 days before the proceeding begins;

(II) the offer is not accepted within 10 days; and

(III) the court or administrative hearing officer finds that the relief finally obtained by the parents is not more favorable to the parents than the offer of settlement.

(ii) Attorneys' fees may not be awarded relating to any meeting of the IEP Team unless such meeting is convened as a result of an administrative proceeding or judicial action, or, at the discretion of the State, for a mediation described in subsection (e) that is prior to the filing of a complaint under subsection (b)(6) or (k) of this section.

(E) Exception to Prohibition on Attorneys' Fees and Related Costs. Notwithstanding subparagraph (D), an award of attorneys' fees and related costs may be made to a parent who is the prevailing party and who was substantially justified in rejecting the settlement offer.

(F) Reduction in Amount of Attorneys' Fees. Except as provided in subparagraph (G), whenever the court finds that—

(i) the parent, during the course of the action or proceeding, unreasonably protracted the final resolution of the controversy;

(ii) the amount of the attorneys' fees otherwise authorized to be awarded unreasonably exceeds the hourly rate prevailing in the community for similar services by attorneys of reasonably comparable skill, reputation, and experience;

(iii) the time spent and legal services furnished were excessive considering the nature of the action or proceeding; or

(iv) the attorney representing the parent did not provide to the school district the appropriate information in the due process complaint in accordance with subsection (b)(7);

the court shall reduce, accordingly, the amount of the attorneys' fees awarded under this section.

(G) Exception to Reduction in Amount of Attorneys' Fees. The provisions of subparagraph (F) shall not apply in any action or proceeding if the court finds that the State or local educational agency unreasonably protracted the final resolution of the action or proceeding or there was a violation of this section.

(j) Maintenance of Current Educational Placement.

Except as provided in subsection (k)(7), during the pendency of any proceedings conducted pursuant to this section, unless the State or local educational agency and the parents otherwise agree, the child shall remain in the then-current educational placement of such child, or, if applying for initial admission to a public school, shall, with the consent of the parents, be placed in the public school program until all such proceedings have been completed.

(k) Placement in Alternative Educational Setting.

(1) Authority of School Personnel.

(A) School personnel under this section may order a change in the placement of a child with a disability—

(i) to an appropriate interim alternative educational setting, another setting, or suspension, for not more than 10 school days (to the extent such alternatives would be applied to children without disabilities); and

(ii) to an appropriate interim alternative educational setting for the same amount of time that a child without a disability would be subject to discipline, but for not more than 45 days if—

(I) the child carries a weapon to school or to a school function under the jurisdiction of a State or a local educational agency; or

(II) the child knowingly possesses or uses illegal drugs or sells or solicits the sale of a controlled substance while at school or a school function under the jurisdiction of a State or local educational agency.

(B) Either before or not later than 10 days after taking a disciplinary action described in subparagraph (A)—

(i) if the local educational agency did not conduct a functional behavioral assessment and implement a behavioral intervention plan for such child before the behavior that resulted in the suspension described in subparagraph (A), the agency shall convene an IEP meeting to develop an assessment plan to address that behavior; or

(ii) if the child already has a behavioral intervention plan, the IEP Team shall review the plan and modify it, as necessary, to address the behavior.

(2) Authority of Hearing Officer. A hearing officer under this section may order a change in the placement of a child with a disability to an appropriate interim alternative educational setting for not more than 45 days if the hearing officer—

(A) determines that the public agency has demonstrated by substantial evidence that maintaining the current placement of such child is substantially likely to result in injury to the child or to others;

(B) considers the appropriateness of the child's current placement;

(C) considers whether the public agency has made reasonable efforts to minimize the risk of harm in the child's current placement, including the use of supplementary aids and services; and

(D) determines that the interim alternative educational setting meets the requirements of paragraph (3)(B).

(3) Determination of Setting.

(A) In General. The alternative educational setting described in paragraph (1)(A)(ii) shall be determined by the IEP Team.

(B) Additional Requirements. Any interim alternative educational setting in which a child is placed under paragraph (1) or (2) shall—

(i) be selected so as to enable the child to continue to participate in the general curriculum, although in another setting, and to continue to receive those services and modifications, including those described in the child's current IEP, that will enable the child to meet the goals set out in that IEP; and

(ii) include services and modifications designed to address the behavior described in paragraph (1) or paragraph (2) so that it does not recur.

(4) Manifestation Determination Review.

(A) In General. If a disciplinary action is contemplated as described in paragraph (1) or paragraph (2) for a behavior of a child with a disability described in either of those paragraphs, or if a disciplinary action involving a change of placement for more than 10 days is contemplated for a child with a disability who has engaged in other behavior that violated any rule or code of conduct of the local educational agency that applies to all children—

(i) not later than the date on which the decision to take that action is made, the parents shall be notified of that decision and of all procedural safeguards accorded under this section; and

(ii) immediately, if possible, but in no case later than 10 school days after the date on which the decision to take that action is made, a review shall be conducted of the relationship between the child's disability and the behavior subject to the disciplinary action.

(B) Individuals to Carry Out Review. A review described in subparagraph (A) shall be conducted by the IEP Team and other qualified personnel.

(C) Conduct of Review. In carrying out a review described in subparagraph (A), the IEP Team may determine that the behavior of the child was not a manifestation of such child's disability only if the IEP Team—

(i) first considers, in terms of the behavior subject to disciplinary action, all relevant information, including—

(I) evaluation and diagnostic results, including such results or other relevant information supplied by the parents of the child;

(II) observations of the child; and

(III) the child's IEP and placement; and

(ii) then determines that—

(I) in relationship to the behavior subject to disciplinary action, the child's IEP and placement were appropriate and the special education services, supplementary aids and services, and behavior intervention strategies were provided consistent with the child's IEP and placement;

(II) the child's disability did not impair the ability of the child to understand the impact and consequences of the behavior subject to disciplinary action; and

(III) the child's disability did not impair the ability of the child to control the behavior subject to disciplinary action.

(5) Determination That Behavior Was Not Manifestation of Disability.

(A) In General. If the result of the review described in paragraph (4) is a determination, consistent with paragraph (4)(C), that the behavior of the child with a disability was not a manifestation of the child's disability, the relevant disciplinary procedures applicable to children without disabilities may be applied to the child in the same manner in which they would be applied to children without disabilities, except as provided in Section 1412(a)(1).

(B) Additional Requirement. If the public agency initiates disciplinary procedures applicable to all children, the agency shall ensure that the special education and disciplinary records of the child with a disability are transmitted for consideration by the person or persons making the final determination regarding the disciplinary action.

(6) Parent Appeal.

(A) In General.

(i) If the child's parent disagrees with a determination that the child's behavior was not a manifestation of the child's disability or with any decision regarding placement, the parent may request a hearing.

(ii) The State or local educational agency shall arrange for an expedited hearing in any case described in this subsection when requested by a parent.

(B) Review of Decision.

(i) In reviewing a decision with respect to the manifestation determination, the hearing officer shall determine whether the public agency has demonstrated that the child's behavior was not a manifestation of such child's disability consistent with the requirements of paragraph (4)(C).

(ii) In reviewing a decision under paragraph (1)(A)(ii) to place the child in an interim alternative educational setting, the hearing officer shall apply the standards set out in paragraph (2).

(7) Placement During Appeals.

(A) In General. When a parent requests a hearing regarding a disciplinary action described in paragraph (1)(A)(ii) or paragraph (2) to challenge the interim alternative educational setting or the manifestation determination, the child shall remain in the interim alternative educational setting pending the decision of the hearing officer or until the expiration of the time period provided for in paragraph (1)(A)(ii) or paragraph (2), whichever occurs first, unless the parent and the State or local educational agency agree otherwise.

(B) Current Placement. If a child is placed in an interim alternative educational setting pursuant to paragraph (1)(A)(ii) or paragraph (2) and school personnel propose to change the child's placement after expiration of the interim alternative placement, during the pendency of any proceeding to challenge the proposed change in placement, the child shall remain in the current placement (the child's placement prior to the interim alternative educational setting), except as provided in subparagraph (C).

(C) Expedited Hearing.

(i) If school personnel maintain that it is dangerous for the child to be in the current placement (placement prior to removal to the interim alternative education setting) during the pendency of the due process proceedings, the local educational agency may request an expedited hearing.

(ii) In determining whether the child may be placed in the alternative educational setting or in another appropriate placement ordered by the hearing officer, the hearing officer shall apply the standards set out in paragraph (2).

(8) Protections for Children Not Yet Eligible for Special Education and Related Services.

(A) In General. A child who has not been determined to be eligible for special education and related services under this part and who has engaged in behavior that violated any rule or code of conduct of the local educational agency, including any behavior described in paragraph (1), may assert any of the protections provided for in this part if the local educational agency had knowledge (as determined in accordance with this paragraph) that the child was a child with a disability before the behavior that precipitated the disciplinary action occurred.

(B) Basis of Knowledge. A local educational agency shall be deemed to have knowledge that a child is a child with a disability if—

(i) the parent of the child has expressed concern in writing (unless the parent is illiterate or has a disability that prevents compliance with the requirements contained in this clause) to personnel of the appropriate educational agency that the child is in need of special education and related services;

(ii) the behavior or performance of the child demonstrates the need for such services;

(iii) the parent of the child has requested an evaluation of the child pursuant to Section 1414; or

(iv) the teacher of the child, or other personnel of the local educational agency, has expressed concern about the behavior or performance of the child to the director of special education of such agency or to other personnel of the agency.

(C) Conditions That Apply if No Basis of Knowledge.

(i) In General. If a local educational agency does not have knowledge that a child is a child with a disability (in accordance with subparagraph (B)) prior to taking disciplinary measures against the child, the child may be subjected to the same disciplinary measures as measures applied to children without disabilities who engaged in comparable behaviors consistent with clause (ii).

(ii) Limitations. If a request is made for an evaluation of a child during the time period in which the child is subjected to disciplinary measures under paragraph (1) or (2), the evaluation shall be conducted in an expedited manner. If the child is determined to be a child with a disability, taking into consideration information from the evaluation conducted by the agency and information provided by the parents, the agency shall provide special education and related services in accordance with the provisions of this part, except that, pending the results of the evaluation, the child shall remain in the educational placement determined by school authorities.

* * *

(m) Transfer of Parental Rights at Age of Majority.

(1) In General. A State that receives amounts from a grant under this part may provide that, when a child with a disability reaches the age of majority under State law (except for a child with a disability who has been determined to be incompetent under State law)—

(A) the public agency shall provide any notice required by this section to both the individual and the parents;

(B) all other rights accorded to parents under this part transfer to the child;

(C) the agency shall notify the individual and the parents of the transfer of rights; and

(D) all rights accorded to parents under this part transfer to children who are incarcerated in an adult or juvenile Federal, State, or local correctional institution.

(2) Special Rule. If, under State law, a child with a disability who has reached the age of majority under State law, who has not been determined to be incompetent, but who is determined not to have the ability to provide informed consent with respect to the educational program of the child, the State shall establish procedures for appointing the parent of the child, or if the parent is not available, another appropriate individual, to represent the educational interests of the child throughout the period of eligibility of the child under this part.

* * *

SUBCHAPTER III—INFANT'S AND TODDLERS WITH DISABILITIES

Section 1431. Findings and Policy.

(a) Findings.

The Congress finds that there is an urgent and substantial need—

(1) to enhance the development of infants and toddlers with disabilities and to minimize their potential for developmental delay;

(2) to reduce the educational costs to our society, including our Nation's schools, by minimizing the need for special education and related services after infants and toddlers with disabilities reach school age;

(3) to minimize the likelihood of institutionalization of individuals with disabilities and maximize the potential for their independently living in society;

(4) to enhance the capacity of families to meet the special needs of their infants and toddlers with disabilities; and

(5) to enhance the capacity of State and local agencies and service providers to identify, evaluate, and meet the needs of historically under-represented populations, particularly minority, low-income, inner-city, and rural populations.

(b) Policy.

It is therefore the policy of the United States to provide financial assistance to States—

(1) to develop and implement a statewide, comprehensive, coordinated, multidisciplinary, interagency system that provides early in-

tervention services for infants and toddlers with disabilities and their families;

(2) to facilitate the coordination of payment for early intervention services from Federal, State, local, and private sources (including public and private insurance coverage);

(3) to enhance their capacity to provide quality early intervention services and expand and improve existing early intervention services being provided to infants and toddlers with disabilities and their families; and

(4) to encourage States to expand opportunities for children under 3 years of age who would be at risk of having substantial developmental delay if they did not receive early intervention services.

* * *

Section 1436. Individualized Family Service Plan.

(a) Assessment and Program Development.

A statewide system described in Section 1433 shall provide, at a minimum, for each infant or toddler with a disability, and the infant's or toddler's family, to receive—

(1) a multidisciplinary assessment of the unique strengths and needs of the infant or toddler and the identification of services appropriate to meet such needs;

(2) a family-directed assessment of the resources, priorities, and concerns of the family and the identification of the supports and services necessary to enhance the family's capacity to meet the developmental needs of the infant or toddler; and

(3) a written individualized family service plan developed by a multidisciplinary team, including the parents, as required by subsection (e).

(b) Periodic Review.

The individualized family service plan shall be evaluated once a year and the family shall be provided a review of the plan at 6-month intervals (or more often where appropriate based on infant or toddler and family needs).

(c) Promptness After Assessment.

The individualized family service plan shall be developed within a reasonable time after the assessment required by subsection (a)(1) is completed. With the parents' consent, early intervention services may commence prior to the completion of the assessment.

(d) Content of Plan.

The individualized family service plan shall be in writing and contain—

(1) a statement of the infant's or toddler's present levels of physical development, cognitive development, communication development, social or emotional development, and adaptive development, based on objective criteria;

(2) a statement of the family's resources, priorities, and concerns relating to enhancing the development of the family's infant or toddler with a disability;

(3) a statement of the major outcomes expected to be achieved for the infant or toddler and the family, and the criteria, procedures, and timelines used to determine the degree to which progress toward achieving the outcomes is being made and whether modifications or revisions of the outcomes or services are necessary;

(4) a statement of specific early intervention services necessary to meet the unique needs of the infant or toddler and the family, including the frequency, intensity, and method of delivering services;

(5) a statement of the natural environments in which early intervention services shall appropriately be provided, including a justification of the extent, if any, to which the services will not be provided in a natural environment;

(6) the projected dates for initiation of services and the anticipated duration of the services;

(7) the identification of the service coordinator from the profession most immediately relevant to the infant's or toddler's or family's needs (or who is otherwise qualified to carry out all applicable responsibilities under this part) who will be responsible for the implementation of the plan and coordination with other agencies and persons; and

(8) the steps to be taken to support the transition of the toddler with a disability to preschool or other appropriate services.

(e) Parental Consent.

The contents of the individualized family service plan shall be fully explained to the parents and informed written consent from the parents shall be obtained prior to the provision of early intervention services described in such plan. If the parents do not provide consent with respect to a particular early intervention service, then the early intervention services to which consent is obtained shall be provided.

* * *

Section 1439. Procedural Safeguards.

(a) Minimum Procedures.

The procedural safeguards required to be included in a statewide system under Section 1435(a)(13) shall provide, at a minimum, the following:

(1) The timely administrative resolution of complaints by parents. Any party aggrieved by the findings and decision regarding an administrative complaint shall have the right to bring a civil action with respect to the complaint in any State court of competent jurisdiction or in a district court of the United States without regard to the amount in controversy. In any action brought under this paragraph, the court shall receive the records of the administrative proceedings, shall hear additional evidence at the request of a party, and, basing its decision on the preponderance of the evidence, shall grant such relief as the court determines is appropriate.

(2) The right to confidentiality of personally identifiable information, including the right of parents to written notice of and written consent to the exchange of such information among agencies consistent with Federal and State law.

(3) The right of the parents to determine whether they, their infant or toddler, or other family members will accept or decline any early intervention service under this part in accordance with State law without jeopardizing other early intervention services under this part.

(4) The opportunity for parents to examine records relating to assessment, screening, eligibility determinations, and the development and implementation of the individualized family service plan.

(5) Procedures to protect the rights of the infant or toddler whenever the parents of the infant or toddler are not known or cannot be found or the infant or toddler is a ward of the State, including the assignment of an individual (who shall not be an employee of the State lead agency, or other State agency, and who shall not be any person, or any employee of a person, providing early intervention services to the infant or toddler or any family member of the infant or toddler) to act as a surrogate for the parents.

(6) Written prior notice to the parents of the infant or toddler with a disability whenever the State agency or service provider proposes to initiate or change or refuses to initiate or change the identification,

evaluation, or placement of the infant or toddler with a disability, or the provision of appropriate early intervention services to the infant or toddler.

(7) Procedures designed to ensure that the notice required by paragraph (6) fully informs the parents, in the parents' native language, unless it clearly is not feasible to do so, of all procedures available pursuant to this section.

(8) The right of parents to use mediation in accordance with Section 1415(e), except that—

(A) any reference in the section to a State educational agency shall be considered to be a reference to a State's lead agency established or designated under Section 1435(a)(10);

(B) any reference in the section to a local educational agency shall be considered to be a reference to a local service provider or the State's lead agency under this part, as the case may be; and

(C) any reference in the section to the provision of free appropriate public education to children with disabilities shall be considered to be a reference to the provision of appropriate early intervention services to infants and toddlers with disabilities.

(b) Services During Pendency of Proceedings.

During the pendency of any proceeding or action involving a complaint by the parents of an infant or toddler with a disability, unless the State agency and the parents otherwise agree, the infant or toddler shall continue to receive the appropriate early intervention services currently being provided or, if applying for initial services, shall receive the services not in dispute.

* * *

Section 1482. Parent Training and Information Centers.

(a) Program Authorized.

The Secretary may make grants to, and enter into contracts and cooperative agreements with, parent organizations to support parent training and information centers to carry out activities under this section.

(b) Required Activities.

Each parent training and information center that receives assistance under this section shall—

(1) provide training and information that meets the training and information needs of parents of children with disabilities living in the

area served by the center, particularly under-served parents and parents of children who may be inappropriately identified;

(2) assist parents to understand the availability of, and how to effectively use, procedural safeguards under this Act, including encouraging the use, and explaining the benefits, of alternative methods of dispute resolution, such as the mediation process described in Section 1415(e);

(3) serve the parents of infants, toddlers, and children with the full range of disabilities;

(4) assist parents to—

(A) better understand the nature of their children's disabilities and their educational and developmental needs;

(B) communicate effectively with personnel responsible for providing special education, early intervention, and related services;

(C) participate in decision-making processes and the development of individualized education programs under part B and individualized family service plans under part C;

(D) obtain appropriate information about the range of options, programs, services, and resources available to assist children with disabilities and their families;

(E) understand the provisions of this Act for the education of, and the provision of early intervention services to, children with disabilities; and

(F) participate in school reform activities;

(5) in States where the State elects to contract with the parent training and information center, contract with State educational agencies to provide, consistent with subparagraphs (B) and (D) of Section 1415(e)(2), individuals who meet with parents to explain the mediation process to them;

(6) network with appropriate clearinghouses, including organizations conducting national dissemination activities under Section 1485(d), and with other national, State, and local organizations and agencies, such as protection and advocacy agencies, that serve parents and families of children with the full range of disabilities; and

(7) annually report to the Secretary on—

(A) the number of parents to whom it provided information and training in the most recently concluded fiscal year; and

(B) the effectiveness of strategies used to reach and serve parents, including under-served parents of children with disabilities.

(c) Optional Activities.

A parent training and information center that receives assistance under this section may—

(1) provide information to teachers and other professionals who provide special education and related services to children with disabilities;

(2) assist students with disabilities to understand their rights and responsibilities under Section 1415(m) on reaching the age of majority; and

(3) assist parents of children with disabilities to be informed participants in the development and implementation of the State's State improvement plan under subpart 1.

(d) Application Requirements.

Each application for assistance under this section shall identify with specificity the special efforts that the applicant will undertake—

(1) to ensure that the needs for training and information of under-served parents of children with disabilities in the area to be served are effectively met; and

(2) to work with community-based organizations.

(e) Distribution of Funds.

(1) In General. The Secretary shall make at least 1 award to a parent organization in each State, unless the Secretary does not receive an application from such an organization in each State of sufficient quality to warrant approval.

(2) Selection Requirement. The Secretary shall select among applications submitted by parent organizations in a State in a manner that ensures the most effective assistance to parents, including parents in urban and rural areas, in the State.

(f) Quarterly Review.

(1) Requirements.

(A) Meetings. The board of directors or special governing committee of each organization that receives an award under this section shall meet at least once in each calendar quarter to review the activities for which the award was made.

(B) Advising Board. Each special governing committee shall directly advise the organization's governing board of its views and recommendations.

(2) Continuation Award. When an organization requests a continuation award under this section, the board of directors or special governing committee shall submit to the Secretary a written review of the parent training and information program conducted by the organization during the preceding fiscal year.

(g) Definition of Parent Organization.

As used in this section, the term parent organization' means a private nonprofit organization (other than an institution of higher education) that—

(1) has a board of directors—

(A) the majority of whom are parents of children with disabilities;

(B) that includes—

(i) individuals working in the fields of special education, related services, and early intervention; and

(ii) individuals with disabilities; and

(C) the parent and professional members of which are broadly representative of the population to be served; or

(2) has—

(A) a membership that represents the interests of individuals with disabilities and has established a special governing committee that meets the requirements of paragraph (1); and

(B) a memorandum of understanding between the special governing committee and the board of directors of the organization that clearly outlines the relationship between the board and the committee and the decision-making responsibilities and authority of each.

Section 1483. Community Parent Resource Centers.

(a) In General.

The Secretary may make grants to, and enter into contracts and cooperative agreements with, local parent organizations to support parent training and information centers that will help ensure that under-served parents of children with disabilities, including low-income parents, parents of children with limited English proficiency, and parents with disabilities, have the training and information they need to enable them to participate effectively in helping their children with disabilities—

(1) to meet developmental goals and, to the maximum extent possible, those challenging standards that have been established for all children; and

(2) to be prepared to lead productive independent adult lives, to the maximum extent possible.

(b) Required Activities.

Each parent training and information center assisted under this section shall—

(1) provide training and information that meets the training and information needs of parents of children with disabilities proposed to be served by the grant, contract, or cooperative agreement;

(2) carry out the activities required of parent training and information centers under paragraphs (2) through (7) of Section 1482(b);

(3) establish cooperative partnerships with the parent training and information centers funded under Section 1482; and

(4) be designed to meet the specific needs of families who experience significant isolation from available sources of information and support.

(c) Definition.

As used is this section, the term `local parent organization' means a parent organization, as defined in Section 1482(g), that either—

(1) has a board of directors the majority of whom are from the community to be served; or

(2) has—

(A) as a part of its mission, serving the interests of individuals with disabilities from such community; and

(B) a special governing committee to administer the grant, contract, or cooperative agreement, a majority of the members of which are individuals from such community.

Section 1484. Technical Assistance for Parent Training and Information Centers.

(a) In General.

The Secretary may, directly or through awards to eligible entities, provide technical assistance for developing, assisting, and coordinating parent training and information programs carried out by parent training and information centers receiving assistance under sections 1482 and 1483.

(b) Authorized Activities.

The Secretary may provide technical assistance to a parent training and information center under this section in areas such as—

(1) effective coordination of parent training efforts;

(2) dissemination of information;

(3) evaluation by the center of itself;

(4) promotion of the use of technology, including assistive technology devices and assistive technology services;

(5) reaching under-served populations;

(6) including children with disabilities in general education programs;

(7) facilitation of transitions from—

(A) early intervention services to preschool;

(B) preschool to school; and

(C) secondary school to post-secondary environments; and

(8) promotion of alternative methods of dispute resolution.

APPENDIX 6:
SELECTED PROVISIONS OF THE FAMILY EDUCATIONAL AND PRIVACY RIGHTS ACT (20 U.S.C. § 1232g; 34 CFR PART 99 FERPA AND REGULATIONS)

THE FAMILY EDUCATIONAL AND PRIVACY RIGHTS ACT (20 U.S.C. § 1232g)

(a) Conditions for availability of funds to educational agencies or institutions; inspection and review of education records; specific information to be made available; procedure for access to education records; reasonableness of time for such access; hearings; written explanations by parents; definitions

(1)(A) No funds shall be made available under any applicable program to any educational agency or institution which has a policy of denying, or which effectively prevents, the parents of students who are or have been in attendance at a school of such agency or at such institution, as the case may be, the right to inspect and review the education records of their children. If any material or document in the education record of a student includes information on more than one student, the parents of one of such students shall have the right to inspect and review only such part of such material or document as relates to such student or to be informed of the specific information contained in such part of such material. Each educational agency or institution shall establish appropriate procedures for the granting of a request by parents for access to the education records of their children within a reasonable period of time, but in no case more than forty-five days after the request has been made.

(B) No funds under any applicable program shall be made available to any State educational agency (whether or not that agency is an educational agency or institution under this section) that has a policy of denying, or effectively prevents, the parents of students the right to inspect and review the education records maintained by the State educational agency on their children who are or have been in attendance at any school of an educational agency or institution that is subject to the provisions of this section.

(C) The first sentence of subparagraph (A) shall not operate to make available to students in institutions of postsecondary education the following materials:

(i) financial records of the parents of the student or any information contained therein;

(ii) confidential letters and statements of recommendation, which were placed in the education records prior to January 1, 1975, if such letters or statements are not used for purposes other than those for which they were specifically intended;

(iii) if the student has signed a waiver of the student's right of access under this subsection in accordance with subparagraph (D), confidential recommendations—

(I) respecting admission to any educational agency or institution,

(II) respecting an application for employment, and

(III) respecting the receipt of an honor or honorary recognition.

(D) A student or a person applying for admission may waive his right of access to confidential statements described in clause (iii) of subparagraph (C), except that such waiver shall apply to recommendations only if (i) the student is, upon request, notified of the names of all persons making confidential recommendations and (ii) such recommendations are used solely for the purpose for which they were specifically intended. Such waivers may not be required as a condition for admission to, receipt of financial aid from, or receipt of any other services or benefits from such agency or institution.

(2) No funds shall be made available under any applicable program to any educational agency or institution unless the parents of students who are or have been in attendance at a school of such agency or at such institution are provided an opportunity for a hearing by such agency or institution, in accordance with regulations of the Secretary, to challenge the content of such student's education records, in order to insure that the records are not inaccurate, misleading, or otherwise in violation of the privacy rights of students, and to provide an opportunity for the correction or deletion of any such inaccurate, misleading or otherwise inappropriate data contained therein

and to insert into such records a written explanation of the parents respecting the content of such records.

(3) For the purposes of this section the term "educational agency or institution" means any public or private agency or institution which is the recipient of funds under any applicable program.

(4)(A) For the purposes of this section, the term "education records" means, except as may be provided otherwise in subparagraph (B), those records, files, documents, and other materials which—

(i) contain information directly related to a student; and

(ii) are maintained by an educational agency or institution or by a person acting for such agency or institution.

(B) The term "education records" does not include—

(i) records of instructional, supervisory, and administrative personnel and educational personnel ancillary thereto which are in the sole possession of the maker thereof and which are not accessible or revealed to any other person except a substitute;

(ii) records maintained by a law enforcement unit of the educational agency or institution that were created by that law enforcement unit for the purpose of law enforcement;

(iii) in the case of persons who are employed by an educational agency or institution but who are not in attendance at such agency or institution, records made and maintained in the normal course of business which relate exclusively to such person in that person's capacity as an employee and are not available for use for any other purpose; or

(iv) records on a student who is eighteen years of age or older, or is attending an institution of postsecondary education, which are made or maintained by a physician, psychiatrist, psychologist— or other recognized professional or paraprofessional acting in his professional or paraprofessional capacity, or assisting in that capacity, and which are made,

maintained, or used only in connection with the provision of treatment to the student, and are not available to anyone other than persons providing such treatment, except that such records can be personally reviewed by a physician or other appropriate professional of the student's choice.

(5)(A) For the purposes of this section the term "directory information" relating to a student includes the following: the student's name, address, telephone listing, date and place of birth, major field of study, participation in officially recognized activities and sports, weight and height of members of athletic teams, dates of attendance, degrees and awards received, and the most recent previous educational agency or institution attended by the student.

(B) Any educational agency or institution making public directory information shall give public notice of the categories of information which it has designated as such information with respect to each student attending the institution or agency and shall allow a reasonable period of time after such notice has been given for a parent to inform the institution or agency that any or all of the information designated should not be released without the parent's prior consent.

(6) For the purposes of this section, the term "student" includes any person with respect to whom an educational agency or institution maintains education records or personally identifiable information, but does not include a person who has not been in attendance at such agency or institution.

(b) Release of education records; parental consent requirement; exceptions; compliance with judicial orders and subpoenas; audit and evaluation of federally-supported education programs; recordkeeping

(1) No funds shall be made available under any applicable program to any educational agency or institution which has a policy or practice of permitting the release of education records (or personally identifiable information contained therein other than directory information, as defined in paragraph (5) of subsection (a) of this section) of students without the written consent of their parents to any individual, agency, or organization, other than to the following—

(A) other school officials, including teachers within the educational institution or local educational agency, who have been determined by such agency or institution to have legitimate educational interests, including the educational interests of the child for whom consent would otherwise be required;

(B) officials of other schools or school systems in which the student seeks or intends to enroll, upon condition that the student's parents be notified of the transfer, receive a copy of the record if desired, and have an opportunity for a hearing to challenge the content of the record;

(C) authorized representatives of (i) the Comptroller General of the United States, (ii) the Secretary, (iii) an administrative head of an education agency (as defined in section 1221e-3(c) of this title), or (iv) State educational authorities under the conditions set forth in paragraph (3) of this subsection;

(D) in connection with a student's application for, or receipt of, financial aid;

(E) State and local officials or authorities to whom such information is specifically allowed to be reported or disclosed pursuant to State statute adopted—

(i) before November 19, 1974, if the allowed reporting or disclosure concerns the juvenile justice system and such system's ability to effectively serve the student whose records are released, or

(ii) after November 19, 1974, if—

(I) the allowed reporting or disclosure concerns the juvenile justice system and such system's ability to effectively serve, prior to adjudication, the student whose records are released; and

(II) the officials and authorities to whom such information is disclosed certify in writing to the educational agency or institution that the information will not be disclosed to any other party except as provided under State law without the prior written consent of the parent of the student.

(F) organizations conducting studies for, or on behalf of, educational agencies or institutions for the purpose of developing, validating, or administering predictive tests, administering student aid programs, and improving instruction, if such studies are conducted in such a manner as will not permit the personal identification of students and their parents by persons other than representatives of such organizations and such information will be destroyed when no longer needed for the purpose for which it is conducted;

(G) accrediting organizations in order to carry out their accrediting functions;

(H) parents of a dependent student of such parents, as defined in section 152 of Title 26;

(I) subject to regulations of the Secretary, in connection with an emergency, appropriate persons if the knowledge of such information is necessary to protect the health or safety of the student or other persons; and

(J)(i) the entity or persons designated in a Federal grand jury subpoena, in which case the court shall order, for good cause shown, the educational agency or institution (and any officer, director, employee, agent, or attorney for such agency or institution) on which the subpoena is served, to not disclose to any person the existence or contents of the subpoena or any information furnished to the grand jury in response to the subpoena; and

(ii) the entity or persons designated in any other subpoena issued for a law enforcement purpose, in which case the court or other issuing agency may order, for good cause shown, the educational agency or institution (and any officer, director, employee, agent, or attorney for such agency or institution) on which the subpoena is served, to not disclose to any person the existence or contents of the subpoena or any information furnished in response to the subpoena.

Nothing in clause (E) of this paragraph shall prevent a State from further limiting the number or type of State or local officials who will continue to have access thereunder.

(2) No funds shall be made available under any applicable program to any educational agency or institution which has a policy or practice of releasing, or providing access to, any personally identifiable information in education records other than directory information, or as is permitted under paragraph (1) of this subsection unless—

(A) there is written consent from the student's parents specifying records to be released, the reasons for such release, and to whom, and with a copy of the records to be released to the student's parents and the student if desired by the parents, or

(B) except as provided in paragraph (1)(J), such information is furnished in compliance with judicial order, or pursuant to any lawfully issued subpoena, upon condition that parents and the students are notified of all such orders or subpoenas in advance of the compliance therewith by the educational institution or agency.

(3) Nothing contained in this section shall preclude authorized representatives of (A) the Comptroller General of the United States, (B) the Secretary, (C) an administrative head of an education agency or (D) State educational authorities from having access to student or other records which may be necessary in connection with the audit and evaluation of Federally supported education program, or in connection with the enforcement of the Federal legal requirements which relate to such programs: provided, That except when collection of personally identifiable information is specifically authorized by Federal law, any data collected by such officials shall be protected in a manner which will not permit the personal identification of students and their parents by other than those officials, and such personally identifiable data shall be destroyed when no longer needed

for such audit, evaluation, and enforcement of Federal legal requirements.

(4)(A) Each educational agency or institution shall maintain a record, kept with the education records of each student, which will indicate all individuals (other than those specified in paragraph (1)(A) of this subsection), agencies, or organizations which have requested or obtained access to a student's education records maintained by such educational agency or institution, and which will indicate specifically the legitimate interest that each such person, agency, or organization has in obtaining this information. Such record of access shall be available only to parents, to the school official and his assistants who are responsible for the custody of such records, and to persons or organizations authorized in, and under the conditions of, clauses (A) and (C) of paragraph (1) as a means of auditing the operation of the system.

(B) With respect to this subsection, personal information shall only be transferred to a third party on the condition that such party will not permit any other party to have access to such information without the written consent of the parents of the student. If a third party outside the educational agency or institution permits access to information in violation of paragraph (2)(A), or fails to destroy information in violation of paragraph (1)(F), the educational agency or institution shall be prohibited from permitting access to information from education records to that third party for a period of not less than five years.

(5) Nothing in this section shall be construed to prohibit State and local educational officials from having access to student or other records which may be necessary in connection with the audit and evaluation of any federally or State supported education program or in connection with the enforcement of the Federal legal requirements which relate to any such program, subject to the conditions specified in the proviso in paragraph (3).

(6)(A) Nothing in this section shall be construed to prohibit an institution of postsecondary education from disclosing, to an alleged victim of any crime of violence (as that term is defined in section 16 of Title 18), or a nonforcible sex offense the final results of any disciplinary proceeding conducted by such institution against the alleged perpetrator of such crime with respect to such crime or offense.

(B) Nothing in this section shall be construed to prohibit an institution of postsecondary education from disclosing the final results of any disciplinary proceeding conducted by such institution against a student who is an alleged perpetrator of any crime of violence (as that term is defined in section 16 of title 18), or a nonforcible sex offense, if the institution determines as a result of that disciplinary proceeding that the student committed a violation of the institution's rules or policies with respect to such crime or offense.

(C) For the purpose of this paragraph, the final results of any disciplinary proceeding—

(i) shall include only the name of the student, the violation committed, and any sanction imposed by the institution on that student; and

(ii) may include the name of any other student, such as a victim or witness, only with the written consent of that other student.

* * *

(c) Surveys or data-gathering activities; regulations

Not later than 240 days after the date of enactment of the Improving America's Schools Act of 1994, the Secretary shall adopt appropriate regulations or procedures, or identify existing regulations or procedures, which protect the rights of privacy of students and their families in connection with any surveys or data-gathering activities conducted, assisted, or authorized by the Secretary or an administrative head of an education agency. Regulations established under this subsection shall include provisions controlling the use, dissemination, and protection of such data. No survey or data-gathering activities shall be conducted by the Secretary, or an administrative head of an education agency under an applicable program, unless such activities are authorized by law.

(d) Students' rather than parents' permission or consent

For the purposes of this section, whenever a student has attained eighteen years of age, or is attending an institution of postsecondary education the permission or consent required of and the rights accorded to the parents of the student shall thereafter only be required of and accorded to the student.

(e) Informing parents or students of rights under this section

No funds shall be made available under any applicable program to any educational agency or institution unless such agency or institution effectively informs the parents of students, or the students, if they are eighteen years of age or older, or are attending an institution of postsecondary education, of the rights accorded them by this section.

(f) Enforcement; termination of assistance

The Secretary, or an administrative head of an education agency, shall take appropriate actions to enforce provisions of this section and to deal with violations of this section, according to the provisions of this chapter, except that action to terminate assistance may be taken only if the Secretary finds there has been a failure to comply with the provisions of this section, and he has determined that compliance cannot be secured by voluntary means.

(g) Office and review board; creation; functions

The Secretary shall establish or designate an office and review board within the Department of Education for the purpose of investigating, processing, reviewing, and adjudicating violations of the provisions of this section and complaints which may be filed concerning alleged violations of this section. Except for the conduct of hearings, none of the functions of the Secretary under this section shall be carried out in any of the regional offices of such Department.

(h) Nothing in this section shall prohibit an educational agency or institution from

(1) including appropriate information in the education record of any student concerning disciplinary action taken against such student for conduct that posed a significant risk to the safety or well-being of that student, other students, or other members of the school community; or

(2) disclosing such information to teachers and school officials, including teachers and school officials in other schools , who have legitimate educational interests in the behavior of the student.

* * *

APPENDIX 7:
SAMPLE EDUCATION DISABILITY
DISCRIMINATION COMPLAINT

Jeffrey P. Foote (Oregon State Bar No. 74098)
Jeffrey Foote & Associates P.C.
Suite 950, 621 S.W. Morrison St.
Portland, OR 92705
Telephone: (503) 228-1133
Facsimile: (503) 228-1556

Sid Wolinsky (California State Bar No. 33716)
Josh Konecky (California State Bar No. 182897)
Alison Aubry (California State Bar No. 194107)

Disability Rights Advocates
449 15th Street, Suite 303
Oakland, CA 94612
Telephone: (510) 451-8644
Facsimile: (510) 451-8511

Adel P. Kimmel (Washington, D.C. Bar No. 412612)
Sarah Posner (Washington, D.C. Bar No. 428015)

Trial Lawyers for Public Justice, P.C.
1717 Massachusetts Ave. N.W., Ste 800
Washington, D.C. 20036
Telephone: (202) 797-8600
Facsimile: (202) 232-7203
Attorneys for Plaintiffs

UNITED STATES DISTRICT COURT - DISTRICT OF OREGON

ADVOCATES FOR SPECIAL KIDS; EDITH WYRICK, by her guardian ad litem Catherine Wood Wyrick; AARON WEINGARTEN, by his guardian ad litem Darlene Weingarten; TARA PETERSON, by her guardian ad litem

Mary Peterson; BRETT McNEIL, by his guardian ad litem Cathie McNeil; and SHEA KEITH IVEY, by his guardian ad litem Cynthia Kay Ivey.

PLAINTIFFS,

- against -

OREGON STATE BOARD OF EDUCATION, an Oregon public entity; WAYNE FELLER, Chair of the Oregon State Board of Education; STAN BUNN, Oregon State Superintendent of Public Instruction; PORTLAND PUBLIC SCHOOLS BOARD OF EDUCATION, a public entity; RON SAXTON, Chair of the Portland Public Schools Board of Education; and BENJAMIN CANADA, Superintendent of Portland Public Schools.

DEFENDANTS.

CASE NO. CV 99-263 KI —CLASS ACTION

COMPLAINT

INTRODUCTORY ALLEGATIONS

1. This action arises out of Defendant OREGON STATE BOARD OF EDUCATION's discrimination against tens of thousands of children with learning disabilities in the Oregon public school system. The Defendant school bureaucracies are, without adequate preparation or safeguards, hastily forcing a testing system upon these children which is destroying and ignoring their educational attainments and self esteem, flagrantly violating their Federal and State rights, and damaging their academic opportunities forever.

2. Learning disabilities describe a range of disabilities which primarily emanate from a neurological or similar defect in the processing of language. In the past, children with learning disabilities were often labeled as slow, not smart or lazy. They are none of these. People with learning disabilities span the intelligence spectrum and many children with learning disabilities are of very high intelligence. Prominent high achieving people with learning disabilities include Charles Schwab, Albert Einstein, Agatha Christie, William Butler Yeats, and John Irving. Many people with learning disabilities work far harder than others in order to compensate for their disabilities. Approximately one half of those with learning disabilities have some form of dyslexia. Dyslexia is a neurological defect in processing phonemes, the basic unit of language, and can be seen in brain scans as early as infancy. Among other things, children with dyslexia are unable to spell due to this neurological defect. *See* Sally E. Shaywitz, Dyslexia, *Scientific American* (Nov. 1996).

3. As part of a radical revision of Oregon's entire educational system, the OREGON STATE BOARD OF EDUCATION has devised and implemented for the first time during the 1998-1999 school year a series of discriminatory, high stakes screening tests that all tenth grade students in Oregon's public schools are required to pass in order to achieve a "Certificate of Initial Mastery" (hereafter the "CIM"). Tenth grade students must first receive the CIM before beginning work towards the Certificate of Advanced Mastery (hereafter the "CAM"), which they must obtain prior to—and in some instances as a condition of—graduation from high school.

4. In formulating and administering the CIM screening tests, the STATE BOARD OF EDUCATION has failed and refused to take account of the needs of children with learning disabilities. As a result, the new exams discriminate against children with learning disabilities in numerous ways. For example, one of the required screening tests, the "direct writing assessment," places twice as much weight (40%) on such factors as spelling and punctuation as on cognitive abilities, organizational skills, or any other element of writing. Children who do not get passing grades on spelling and punctuation will fail the test no matter how intelligent, knowledgeable, and academically gifted they are, or how high they score on other parts of the test.

5. The action of the STATE BOARD OF EDUCATION in making elements such as spelling and punctuation twice as important as ideas, content and organization was a political and arbitrary act without any sound basis in valid test construction procedures.

6. Children with dyslexia and other learning disabilities who are unable to spell due to neurological deficiencies will not pass the writing test (and therefore will not achieve a Certificate of Initial Mastery). In effect, Defendants have made the ability to spell well a prerequisite to academic advancement in the Oregon public education system, even though there is no major university in America that requires proficiency in spelling as an admission requirement.

7. Defendants are required under federal law to provide reasonable accommodations to children with disabilities on the screening tests. In flagrant violation of that requirement, the STATE BOARD OF EDUCATION has failed to articulate or implement any coherent policy regarding providing reasonable accommodations on the screening tests.

8. Through ad hoc decision making, Defendant bureaucracies have created chaos and confusion among parents, children and educators by providing ambiguous, conflicting and misleading information regarding the policies and procedures for obtaining accommodations on the statewide screening tests.

9. Up to the very day the writing exam was being given, high ranking bureaucrats in the Oregon Department of Education provided directly contradictory information to parents about how the high stakes tests were to be administered and graded for disabled children. *See* Exhibit A to Complaint. Some parents were told that their child could not use a reasonable accommodation such as a word processor with a spell-check program on the writing test, regardless of the child's individual disability and particular needs. Other parents were told that their child could use a word processor with a spell-check program, but that the use of a word processor was a "modification" that would invalidate the results of the test. Still other parents were told that their child could use a word processor, without any information whatsoever about the possible detrimental consequences of using such a "modification."

10. Not only do the Defendant bureaucracies not have a single, understandable policy regarding the provision of accommodations on these high stakes exams, but they have engaged in a semantic game in which they have re-labeled reasonable accommodations as "modifications" in an effort to avoid their legal obligations. As a result of the confusion created by the Defendant bureaucracies, parents have been unable to make informed choices regarding the accommodations that their children can use on the statewide screening tests.

11. During the administration of the CIM screening tests, Defendants refused to provide numerous children with learning disabilities reasonable accommodations such as word processors with spell-check programs, despite the fact that such spell-check programs are now universally used by college students, the business, professional and academic communities, and any place the English language is written. By prohibiting the use of word processors with spell-check programs, Defendants have violated their own mandate of treating the use of technology as an integral part of the educational process.

12. Defendants are fully aware that for many children with learning disabilities, the denial of a reasonable accommodation such as a word processor virtually guarantees that the child will fail the writing test. By testing the child's disability and requiring them to fail, Defendant STATE BOARD OF EDUCATION is effectively refusing to recognize all of the abilities and attainments of the disabled child, no matter how extensive those may be.

13. Some children with learning disabilities used word processors with spell-check programs during the CIM screening tests, mistakenly believing—due to Defendants' affirmative misrepresentations and misinformation—that these "modified" tests will count towards achieving the Certificate of Initial Mastery. Even if these children receive passing scores on the CIM tests, however, Defendants will not allow them to

achieve a Certificate of Initial Mastery because they used a "modification" during the test.

14. The consequences to children of failing to receive a Certificate of Initial Mastery are profound. In addition to the damage to their self-esteem, these children may be required to repeat tenth grade, may be excluded from participating in their school's honors programs, may receive a lesser "modified" diploma, may not graduate from high school, may not be able to gain admission to Oregon's public universities and community colleges, and will be severely disadvantaged in applying for employment. In addition, parents are reasonably concerned that their children with learning disabilities will be frustrated, discouraged and drastically set back in their educational advancement.

15. By requiring children with learning disabilities to take discriminatory and unfair tests with high stakes consequences and no reasonable accommodations, the STATE BOARD OF EDUCATION has created a dual track system of public education in which children with learning disabilities will be relegated to the lower tier and prevented from pursuing academic opportunities simply because of their disabilities.

16. The high stakes screening tests further discriminate against children with learning disabilities because these children have not been prepared by their administrators or teachers to take the Certificate of Initial Mastery tests. Throughout their educations, these children have received as part of their legally mandated Individual Educational Programs (or "Section 504" education plans) accommodations such as word processors with automatic spell-checkers. Now, for the first time in tenth grade, children are tested on skills that they do not possess neurologically. Moreover, these children have never been provided with any instruction on how to compensate for these deficits in testing situations.

17. The high stakes screening tests, with their unvalidated over-emphasis on spelling and punctuation, will also damage the educational opportunities of minority children, children of immigrants, and children for whom English is not their primary language.

18. Past experience with tests like those required for the CIM and CAM, coupled with Defendants' incompetent administration of those tests, make it likely that a great majority of Oregon students with learning disabilities will not be able to ever obtain a CIM or CAM.

19. Without immediate relief from the Court, Plaintiff children will be irreparably harmed in that they will be denied numerous academic opportunities, may not graduate from high school, and will experience severe damage to their self-esteem and emotional well-being.

JURISDICTION

20. The Court has subject matter jurisdiction over the federal law claims under 28 U.S.C. §§ 1331 and 1343. The Court has jurisdiction over the Oregon law claims under the doctrine of supplemental jurisdiction pursuant to 28 U.S.C. § 1367.

21. The Court has jurisdiction to issue a declaratory judgment pursuant to 28 U.S.C. §§ 2201 and 2202.

22. Plaintiffs have no adequate remedy at law to compensate them for the deprivation of educational and professional opportunities they will suffer as a result of the OREGON STATE BOARD OF EDUCATION's discriminatory actions. Defendants have a clear and mandatory legal duty to administer its public school system in a manner consistent with all applicable laws. Plaintiffs will suffer irreparable harm without immediate injunctive relief.

23. Plaintiffs are not required to exhaust the administrative procedures set forth in IDEA because they are challenging policies and practices of general applicability that are contrary to numerous Federal and State laws (including IDEA) and because Plaintiffs cannot obtain adequate relief through administrative remedies.

VENUE

24. Venue is proper in this Court under 28 U.S.C. § 1391(b). All Defendants reside in the State of Oregon, Defendants PORTLAND PUBLIC SCHOOLS BOARD OF EDUCATION, RON SAXTON, and BENJAMIN CANADA reside in Portland, and a substantial part of the events giving rise to this action occurred in Portland.

THE PARTIES

25. Plaintiff ADVOCATES FOR SPECIAL KIDS ("ASK") is an organization comprised of parents of children with learning disabilities who attend Oregon public schools. The mission of ASK is to fight for the enforcement of educational rights of children with disabilities.

26. Plaintiff EDITH WYRICK, by her guardian ad litem CATHERINE WOOD WYRICK, is a citizen of the United States and resides in the City of Portland. Plaintiff is 15 years old and in ninth grade at Wilson High School in Portland. She has a learning disability, and is a qualified person with a disability within the meaning of applicable Federal and State law.

27. Plaintiff AARON WEINGARTEN, by his guardian ad litem DARLENE WEINGARTEN, is a citizen of the United States and resides in the City of Portland. Plaintiff is 15 years old and in tenth grade at Wilson High School in Portland. He has a learning disability, and is a qualified per-

son with a disability within the meaning of applicable Federal and State law.

28. Plaintiff TARA PETERSON, by her guardian MARY PETERSON, is a United States citizen and a resident of the City of Portland. Plaintiff is 15 years old and in tenth grade at Wilson High School in Portland. She has a learning disability and is a qualified person with a disability within the meaning of applicable Federal and State law.

29. Plaintiff BRETT McNEIL, by his guardian ad litem CATHIE McNEIL is a citizen of the United States and resides in the City of Portland. Plaintiff is 16 years old and in the tenth grade at Wilson High School in Portland. He has a learning disability and is a qualified person with a disability within the meaning of applicable Federal and State law.

30. Plaintiff SHEA KEITH IVEY, by his guardian ad litem CYNTHIA KAY IVEY, is a citizen of the United States and resides in the City of Portland. Plaintiff is 13 years old and in eighth grade at West Sylvan Middle School in Portland. He has a learning disability, and is a qualified person with a disability within the meaning of applicable Federal and State law.

31. Defendant OREGON STATE BOARD OF EDUCATION ("STATE BOARD") is a public entity within the meaning of Title II of the Americans with Disabilities Act and other applicable laws. The STATE BOARD receives Federal financial assistance from the Department of Education and is therefore covered by the requirements of Section 504 of the Rehabilitation Act of 1973. The STATE BOARD is a state educational agency and is therefore covered by the requirements of the Individuals with Disabilities Education Act.

32. Defendant WAYNE FELLER is the Chair of the OREGON STATE BOARD OF EDUCATION. He is sued in his official capacity.

33. Defendant STAN BUNN is the Oregon State Superintendent of Public Instruction. He is sued in his official capacity.

34. Defendant PORTLAND PUBLIC SCHOOLS BOARD OF EDUCATION formulates policies for the Portland Public Schools. The PORTLAND PUBLIC SCHOOLS BOARD OF EDUCATION is a public entity within the meaning of Title II of the Americans with Disabilities Act, and receives Federal financial assistance from the Department of Education and is therefore covered by the requirements of Section 504 of the Rehabilitation Act of 1973. The PORTLAND PUBLIC SCHOOLS BOARD OF EDUCATION is a local educational agency and is therefore covered by the requirements of the Individuals with Disabilities Education Act.

35. Defendant RON SAXTON is the Chair of the PORTLAND PUBLIC SCHOOLS BOARD OF EDUCATION. He is sued in his official capacity.

36. Defendant BENJAMIN CANADA is the Superintendent of Portland Public Schools. He is sued in his official capacity.

FACTUAL ALLEGATIONS

37. Plaintiffs, who attend public schools throughout Oregon, are children with learning disabilities. Learning disabilities are the result of permanent neurological dysfunction or information processing disruptions that result in limited, unexpected, and usually intractable impediments in the ability to learn one or more basic skills taught through traditional formal education.

38. There are currently tens of thousands of children with identified learning disabilities who attend Oregon's public schools. There are also many children with learning disabilities who attend Oregon's public schools who have not yet been identified as learning disabled for a number of reasons. In many cases, the school and/or school district has not adequately assessed the child to determine if he or she has a learning disability. In other instances, children have not been identified as learning disabled because their particular learning disabilities have not affected their educational performance or attainments thus far.

39. People with learning disabilities span the intelligence spectrum and many children with learning disabilities are of very high intelligence. Many people with learning disabilities work far harder than others in order to compensate for their disabilities.

40. In 1991, the Oregon State Legislature passed the Oregon Educational Act for the 21st Century ("the Act"). O.R.S. § 329, *et seq.* The Act radically restructures public education in the State of Oregon. A central component of this restructuring is the establishment of, in addition to the standard diploma, the "Certificate of Initial Mastery" ("CIM") to be earned by all tenth grade students in the public schools, and the "Certificate of Advanced Mastery" ("CAM") to be earned by all twelfth grade students attending public schools.

41. The Act directs the OREGON STATE BOARD OF EDUCATION to prescribe the standards that a student must meet in order to obtain Certificates of Initial and Advanced Mastery. Pursuant to this authority, the STATE BOARD has created a series of high stakes screening tests that children must take and pass during their tenth grade year to achieve a CIM. The STATE BOARD is currently formulating the tests that twelfth grade students will need to take and pass to achieve a CAM.

42. In devising these tests and formulating the standards that students must meet in order to obtain a CIM, the STATE BOARD failed to consider and take account of the needs of children with learning dis-

abilities (and children for whom English is not their primary language). As a result, the tests are discriminatory, arbitrary and unfair because the STATE BOARD OF EDUCATION failed to minimize the effects of a child's learning disability. Under federal law, when a test is administered to a child with a learning disability, the test results must accurately reflect the child's aptitude, achievement, or whatever factor the test purports to measure, rather than reflecting the child's learning disability. Contrary to this mandate, the STATE BOARD OF EDUCATION has constructed a screening test which maximizes the effects of children's learning disabilities.

43. None of the Defendants have conducted any study concerning whether or not the skills measured on the tests were in fact taught to the tens of thousands of students with learning disabilities in the Oregon school system.

44. The 1998-1999 school year is the first year that tenth grade students in Oregon's public schools are required to obtain the CIM. To achieve the CIM during the 1998-1999 school year, students must take a series of English and mathematics tests. The English tests include "reading/literature multiple choice" and "direct writing assessment." The math tests include "mathematics problem solving" (also referred to as "open-ended math") and "math multiple choice." To obtain a CIM, a student must receive passing scores on all of the English and math tests.

45. During the 1998-1999 school year, the CIM screening tests will also be administered to children in the eighth grade to assess these students' progress toward achieving a CIM. Children who do poorly on the CIM tests in eighth grade may be required to repeat eighth grade or attend summer school.

46. The CIM English and math tests discriminate against children with learning disabilities in numerous ways. For example, children are required to handwrite their answers to the writing assessment and the mathematics problem solving tests. The requirement that tests be handwritten unfairly discriminates against children who may excel in ideas, content, organization, fluency and intelligence, but whose learning disabilities impair their ability to express thoughts on paper or impair the act of writing itself.

47. The math problem solving test is also constructed and administered in such a way that it tests language elements such that children with learning disabilities are unfairly disadvantaged.

48. The reading/literature multiple choice test, as currently constructed and administered, unfairly disadvantages children with dyslexia and other reading disabilities.

49. The writing test, as currently formulated and administered, further discriminates against children with learning disabilities because it places an unreasonable, unjustified and unvalidated emphasis on "conventions" such as spelling and punctuation, which account for forty percent (40%) of a child's score on the writing test.

50. In order to pass the writing test, a child (in addition to achieving a high overall score on the writing test) must, as arbitrarily determined by the STATE BOARD, obtain high scores in spelling and punctuation. Because the exam directly test the impairments caused by dyslexia and other learning disorders, the direct writing assessment will be extraordinarily difficult, if not impossible, for people with dyslexia and other learning disabilities to pass, regardless of how intelligent, studied, creative or otherwise gifted they may be.

51. Plaintiff children require (and are guaranteed under federal law) reasonable accommodations on the CIM tests to minimize the effects of their learning disabilities, and without such accommodations, Plaintiff children are subjected to discrimination on the basis of their disabilities. Without reasonable accommodations on the CIM tests, Plaintiff children will be unable to pass the high stakes CIM tests and therefore will be unable to obtain a Certificate of Initial Mastery.

52. The consequences of failing to obtain a Certificate of Initial Mastery are so severe as to permanently alter the entire course of a child's education and future employment no matter how bright the child is or how hard the child has worked. According to the STATE BOARD, schools may consider the failure to achieve a CIM as a factor in deciding whether to require a child to repeat a year of school.

53. Children who do not do well on the CIM tests due to their learning disabilities will also be barred from pursuing academic opportunities. For example, students who attend Wilson High School in Portland are unable to enroll in accelerated English classes unless they have a high—not merely passing—score on the CIM writing test. *See* Exhibit B to Complaint. In order to graduate with honors from Wilson High School, a student must take accelerated English. In effect, children with learning disabilities who cannot pass the CIM writing test due to a lack of reasonable accommodation could be completely shut out of participating in the honors program at Wilson High School. Upon information and belief, other public high schools throughout Oregon are implementing similar requirements with regard to their honors programs. Defendant bureaucracies have undertaken no study justifying the use of spelling and punctuation as prerequisites to enrollment in academic courses.

54. There are numerous other negative and often devastating consequences to failing to achieve a CIM. A student must first achieve a Certificate of Initial Mastery before beginning work on obtaining the Certificate of Advanced Mastery during the twelfth grade. Some Oregon schools require successful achievement of the Certificate of Advanced Mastery in order to graduate from high school. Thus, children who are unable to obtain the CIM will not be able to achieve the CAM, and may not graduate from high school.

55. Children who attend high schools that do not require the CIM or CAM for graduation will be nevertheless severely disadvantaged because Oregon's public universities and community colleges are aligning admission requirements with the CIM and CAM. Accordingly, a child who has not passed the CIM may be barred from admission to public colleges and universities.

56. Many Oregon employers will ask whether job applicants have a CIM or CAM, and may require these certificates as a condition of employment.

57. Defendant bureaucracies have created chaos and confusion by failing to formulate clear policies and procedures regarding the provision of reasonable accommodations on the CIM screening tests. This failure has led to ad hoc policymaking by Defendants and Defendant bureaucracies, resulting in innumerable different "policies" and "procedures." Although the Oregon Department of Education has engaged in an extensive media campaign to promote the CIM and has disseminated numerous documents to parents, students and educators regarding the CIM, there is not a single official document that clearly states the policies and procedures for obtaining reasonable accommodations on the CIM tests. Instead, documents either make no reference whatsoever to the provision of reasonable accommodations for students with disabilities, or the documents contain ambiguous and general statements of policy that provide no meaningful details.

58. Defendants have caused further confusion among parents and educators by arbitrarily re-naming certain accommodations as "modifications" on the CIM screening tests. On numerous documents distributed to schools, educators, parents, and children, the Defendant bureaucracies have listed allowable "accommodations" and "modifications" that children with disabilities may use when taking the CIM screening tests. However, on none of these documents do the Defendant bureaucracies explain what the difference is between an "accommodation" and a "modification," nor do the documents state what the consequences are of taking the tests with an "accommodation" or a "modification."

59. For example, Defendant STATE BOARD OF EDUCATION has determined, without any lawful basis whatsoever, that a word processor with an automatic spell-check function is a "modification," while extended time on tests is an "accommodation." The distinction between a "modification" and an "accommodation," and the consequences that flow from taking a "modified" test, are incomprehensible to parents. These distinctions and consequences also vary depending on which Defendant bureaucracy or school official is dealing with the issue.

60. As a result of the conflicting, confusing and misleading information they have received about the policies and procedures, if any, for obtaining reasonable accommodations, parents of Plaintiff children (a) have been unable to make informed decisions about how the child should approach or take the tests, (b) have been misled about the procedures and consequences, (c) have made decisions which may be unnecessarily damaging to their children's future and (d) have been discouraged from requesting the reasonable accommodations to which they are entitled as a matter of law.

61. As another consequence of the lack of policies and procedures for providing reasonable accommodations on the CIM tests, Plaintiffs and their parents have been unable to participate meaningfully in designing Plaintiffs' Individual Educational Plans or Section 504 Education Plans. By virtue of their disabilities, all Plaintiffs have either a legally mandated Individual Education Plan ("IEP") pursuant to IDEA, or a Section 504 Education Plan ("504 Plan") pursuant to Section 504 of the Rehabilitation Act of 1973. These plans are required by law to be created through an interactive process between educators, parents and their children, and the plans are supposed to specify a child's individual needs.

62. Although Defendant bureaucracies have stated that children will be provided reasonable accommodations in accordance with their IEPs or 504 Plans, this simply has not occurred. In many instances, the issue of reasonable accommodations on the CIM screening tests was not even addressed at the child's IEP or Section 504 meeting.

63. In other instances, although the issue of reasonable accommodations on the CIM tests may have been discussed at a child's IEP or 504 Plan meeting, parents of Plaintiff children were nevertheless unable to make informed choices regarding their child's education because school officials did not know what the policies and procedures were regarding reasonable accommodations on the CIM screening tests, nor did school officials know what the consequences were of taking a "modified" test.

64. At various times, various school officials have made the following representations to parents of Plaintiff children:

Plaintiff EDITH WYRICK's mother and guardian ad litem CATHERINE WOOD WYRICK was told by a representative of the State Department of Education in a public meeting that her daughter could take the CIM writing test with a word processor and an automatic spell-check program, and that such an accommodation was considered a "modification." When Plaintiff EDITH WYRICK's mother inquired as to the meaning of a "modification," she was told that "modifications" alter what the exam is testing and that she would not be able to receive a CIM as a result of having taken a "modified" exam. At that same meeting, Plaintiff EDITH WYRICK's mother was told by school officials that she "would have to litigate the issue." In the fall of 1998, CATHERINE WOOD WYRICK attended her daughter's IEP meeting. At that meeting, school officials told CATHERINE WOOD WYRICK that the use of a computer with a spell-check function on the CIM writing test was considered a "modification." When CATHERINE WOOD WYRICK asked about the consequence of taking the CIM tests with a "modification," the school officials stated that they did not know. In February 1999, after the CIM tests had been administered, CATHERINE WOOD WYRICK was informed by officials at the Department of Education that the use of an "automated correction" spell check feature is a "modification" that "may affect" her daughter's eligibility to receive a CIM. *See* Exhibit C to Complaint.

Plaintiff AARON WEINGARTEN's mother and guardian ad litem DARLENE WEINGARTEN was initially told by the curriculum vice principal at Wilson High School that her son would be able to use a word processor on the CIM tests due to the documentation of Plaintiff WEINGARTEN's disability. DARLENE WEINGARTEN later learned that the special education instructor at Wilson High School told Plaintiff WEINGARTEN that he would not be allowed to use a word processor or spell-checker because he would receive a "modified" CIM. This conflicting information made Plaintiff WEINGARTEN quite anxious and confused. One day before the CIM tests were administered, DARLENE WEINGARTEN was advised by Wilson High School officials that the school officials had just learned that any and all "accommodations" would be considered "modifications" and that if Plaintiff WEINGARTEN used a computer on the tests he would receive a "modified" CIM, regardless of his level of performance on any of the CIM tests. Due to confusion regarding the administration and grading of the CIM tests as well as other health problems, Plaintiff WEINGARTEN did not take the CIM tests.

Plaintiff TARA PETERSON's mother and guardian ad litem MARY PE-TERSON did not receive any information about policies and procedures for requesting reasonable accommodations on the CIM tests. At her daughter's Section 504 meeting during the fall of 1998, the issue of accommodations or "modifications" on the CIM tests was not discussed.

Plaintiff BRETT McNEIL's mother and guardian ad litem CATHIE McNEIL was initially told that her son could use a computer with a spell-checker and grammar-checker on the CIM tests as an "accommodation." Two days later, school administrators told her that the school district considered the use of a computer a "modification" which would negate the results of the test. Most recently, CATHIE McNEIL was told that her son could use a computer on the CIM tests as an "accommodation" and that the tests would "count." Plaintiff McNEIL used a computer on the CIM writing test.

Plaintiff SHEA KEITH IVEY's mother and guardian ad litem CYNTHIA KAY IVEY did not receive any information regarding the policies and procedures for providing reasonable accommodations on the CIM tests, and was unable to find any school official who could answer her questions regarding the difference between an "accommodation" and a "modification" on the CIM tests.

65. Defendants have failed to establish a procedure for challenging even the most arbitrary conduct with regard to the denial of reasonable accommodations.

66. Defendants have failed to provide mechanisms, procedures, policies or personnel to engage in the legally required interactive process with parents and children for the fashioning of reasonable accommodations.

67. Defendants have failed to deal with students on an individualized basis, instead devising and implementing discriminatory across-the-board policies which deny children their legally required reasonable accommodations. Defendants have instituted and are systemically carrying out a pattern and practice of refusing to honor the obligations to provide reasonable accommodations contained in the IEPs or Section 504 Plans of children with learning disabilities.

68. The CIM screening tests discriminate against children with learning disabilities because they test children on material they have never been taught. Upon information and belief, many, if not most, Oregon public schools have not taught students spelling, instead utilizing a "whole language" approach in which spelling is de-emphasized. Thus, Plaintiff children have never been taught spelling and many of the other skills tested on the CIM screening exams.

69. The CIM screening tests have been implemented prematurely. Students with learning disabilities have not been given adequate time and notice to prepare for these new testing requirements. Throughout their educations, Plaintiff children have been provided with reasonable accommodations such as word processors with spell-check programs in accordance with their IEPs or 504 Plans. Defendants have not created any materials or programs for teaching children with learning disabilities what they need to know to pass either the CIM or CAM screening tests without the reasonable accommodations that they have been allowed to utilize throughout the educations.

70. Without immediate relief from the Court, Plaintiff children will be irreparably harmed in that they will be denied numerous academic opportunities, may not graduate from high school, and will experience severe damage to their self-esteem and emotional well-being.

CLASS ALLEGATIONS

71. Plaintiffs bring this action on their own behalf and on behalf of all persons similarly situated. The class which these Plaintiffs represent is composed of all children with diagnosed learning disabilities attending Oregon public schools who have been injured in their legal rights or are threatened with such injury because of Defendants' conduct in establishing and implementing a discriminatory policy against children with learning disabilities as alleged in this Complaint. The class is sometimes hereafter referred to as "Plaintiff children."

72. The persons in the class are so numerous that joinder of all such persons is impracticable and the disposition of their claims in a class action is a benefit to the parties and to the Court.

73. There is a well defined community of interest in the questions of law and fact affecting the class in that they were all discriminated against by the implementation of the new policies against children with learning disabilities. Defendants have acted on grounds applicable to the class as a whole.

74. Common questions of law and fact predominate.

75. The claims of the named Plaintiffs are typical of those of the class, and named Plaintiffs will fairly and adequately represent the interests of the class.

76. References to Plaintiffs shall be deemed to include the named plaintiffs and each member of the class.

FIRST CLAIM

VIOLATIONS OF THE AMERICANS WITH DISABILITIES ACT (42 U.S.C. § 12101 *et seq.*)

77. Plaintiffs incorporate by reference herein the allegations in paragraphs 1 through 76 inclusive.

78. Defendants' acts and omissions alleged herein are in violation of the Americans with Disabilities Act, 42 U.S.C. § 12101, *et seq.*, ("ADA") and the regulations promulgated thereunder, 28 C.F.R. Part 35, *et seq.*

79. Plaintiffs are qualified individuals with disabilities within the meaning of the ADA. 42 U.S.C. § 12131(2).

80. Defendants OREGON STATE BOARD OF EDUCATION and PORT-LAND PUBLIC SCHOOLS BOARD OF EDUCATION are public entities within the meaning of Title II of the ADA and the regulations promulgated thereunder. 42 U.S.C. § 12131(1)(B).

81. In violation of the ADA, Defendant bureaucracies have failed to evaluate their policies and practices to ensure that these policies and procedures do not exclude or limit the participation of individuals with disabilities in their programs and activities, and Defendant bureaucracies have failed to seek public comment regarding the impact of the CIM screening tests and attendant policies and procedures on children with disabilities. 28 C.F.R. § 35.105.

82. By denying Plaintiff children the accommodations they are legally entitled to, Defendant bureaucracies have denied Plaintiffs a free and appropriate education in violation of the ADA. 28 C.F.R. § 35.130; 28 C.F.R. § 35.103(a).

83. In violation of the ADA, Defendant bureaucracies have excluded Plaintiff children from participation in and denied the benefits of the services, programs or activities of a public entity solely on the basis of disability. Defendants have further violated the ADA by otherwise subjecting Plaintiff children to discrimination based upon disability. 42 U.S.C. § 12132; 28 C.F.R. § 35.130(a).

84. Defendant bureaucracies have violated the ADA by denying Plaintiff children the opportunity to participate in or benefit from aids, benefits and services provided by the public entities, and by providing Plaintiff children with the opportunity to participate in or benefit from aids, benefits or services that are not equal to those afforded non-disabled children who attend Oregon's public schools. 28 C.F.R. § 35.130(b)(1)(i)-(ii).

85. Defendant bureaucracies have violated the ADA by providing Plaintiff children with benefits that are different and/or not as effective in

affording equal opportunity to obtain the same results, to gain the same benefits, or to reach the same levels of achievement as that provided to others. 28 C.F.R. § 35.130(b)(1)(iii)(iv).

86. Defendant bureaucracies have violated the ADA by utilizing criteria or methods of administration that have the effect of subjecting Plaintiff children to discrimination on the basis of disability or that have the purpose or effect of defeating or substantially impairing accomplishment of the objectives of the public entity's program with respect to individuals with disabilities. 28 C.F.R. § 35.130(b)(3).

87. Defendant bureaucracies have violated the ADA by administering a certification program in a manner that subjects Plaintiff children to discrimination on the basis of disability. 28 C.F.R. § 35.130(b)(6).

88. Defendant bureaucracies have violated the ADA by failing to make reasonable modifications in policies, practices or procedures when the modifications are necessary to avoid discrimination on the basis of disability. 28 C.F.R. § 35.130(7).

89. Defendant bureaucracies have violated the ADA by imposing eligibility requirements that screen out or tends to screen out an individual with a disability or any class of individuals with disabilities from fully and equally enjoying any service, program, or activity offered by Defendants. 28 C.F.R. § 130.(b)(8).

90. WHEREFORE, Plaintiffs request relief as set forth below.

SECOND CLAIM

VIOLATIONS OF THE REHABILITATION ACT OF 1973 (29 U.S.C. § 794, et seq.)

91. Plaintiffs incorporate by reference herein the allegations in paragraphs 1 through 90 inclusive.

92. Plaintiffs are qualified individuals with disabilities within the meaning the Rehabilitation Act of 1973.

93. Defendants are the recipients of federal funds sufficient to invoke the coverage of the Rehabilitation Act of 1973.

94. Solely by reason of their disabilities, Plaintiffs have been, and continue to be, excluded from participation in, denied the benefits of, and subjected to discrimination in their attempts to receive, full and equal access to the programs, services and activities offered by Defendants in violation of the Rehabilitation Act. 29 U.S.C. § 794; 34 C.F.R. § 104.4(a).

95. Defendant bureaucracies have violated the Rehabilitation Act by denying Plaintiff children the opportunity to participate in or benefit

from aids, benefits and services provided by Defendants, and by providing Plaintiff children with the opportunity to participate in or benefit from aids, benefits or services that are not equal to those afforded non-disabled children who attend Oregon's public schools. 34 C.F.R. § 104.4(b)(1)(i)-(ii).

96. Defendant bureaucracies have violated the Rehabilitation Act by utilizing criteria or methods of administration that have the effect of subjecting Plaintiff children to discrimination on the basis of disability or that have the purpose or effect of defeating or substantially impairing accomplishment of the objectives of Defendants' programs with respect to individuals with disabilities. 34 C.F.R. § 104.4(b)(4).

97. Defendants have failed to provide Plaintiff children with a free and appropriate education in designed to meet their individual educational needs in violation of the Rehabilitation Act. 34 C.F.R. § 104.33(b).

98. The STATE BOARD's sweeping policy precluding the use of accommodations on the statewide exams is in violation of the obligations imposed by the Rehabilitation Act to provide special education and related services in conformity with a child's Section 504 Plan. By imposing a discriminatory, across the board policy to all children with learning disabilities, Defendant bureaucracies have eliminated the individual assessment of children required by the Rehabilitation Act. 34 C.F.R. § 104.33.

99. Defendants have failed to ensure that the statewide screening tests and other evaluation materials have been validated for the specific purpose for which they are used in violation of the Rehabilitation Act. 34 C.F.R. § 104.35(b)(1).

100. Defendants have failed to ensure that the statewide screening tests are administered such that the results will accurately reflect the child's aptitude or achievement level rather than the child's impaired sensory, manual or speaking skills. 34 C.F.R. § 104.35(b)(3).

101. WHEREFORE, Plaintiffs request relief as set forth below.

THIRD CLAIM

VIOLATION OF 42 U.S.C. § 1983 BASED UPON DEPRIVATION OF RIGHTS UNDER THE IDEA

102. Plaintiffs incorporate by reference herein the allegations in paragraphs 1 through 101 inclusive.

103. Defendants' acts and omissions alleged herein are in violation of 42 U.S.C. § 1983 based upon Defendants' violation of the provisions of the Individuals with Disabilities Education Act, 20 U.S.C. § 1400, *et seq.* ("IDEA").

104. At all times mentioned herein, Defendants, and each of them, in administering and failing to lawfully administer the public school system, was acting under color of State law. Defendants have adopted a policy of discrimination based solely upon the disabilities of school children. This policy, conduct, and practice of Defendants has resulted in severe interference with and deprivation of Plaintiffs' fundamental right to a free and appropriate public education which is secured to them by the laws of the United States and specifically pursuant to IDEA. 20 U.S.C. § 1401(8).

105. The STATE BOARD's sweeping policy precluding the use of accommodations on the statewide exams is in violation of the obligations imposed by IDEA to provide special education and related services in conformity with a child's Individualized Education Program ("IEP"). 20 U.S.C. § 1401(8)(D). By imposing a discriminatory, across the board policy to all children with learning disabilities, Defendant bureaucracies have eliminated the individual assessment of children required by IDEA. 20 U.S.C. § 1414.

106. Defendant bureaucracies have violated IDEA by failing to provide appropriate accommodations to children with disabilities on the statewide screening tests. 20 U.S.C. § 1412(a)(17)(A).

107. Defendant bureaucracies have violated IDEA by failing to develop guidelines for the participation of children with disabilities in alternate assessments for those children who cannot participate in statewide assessment programs. 20 U.S.C. § 1412(a)(17)(A)(I).

108. Defendant bureaucracies have violated IDEA by not ensuring that the statewide screening tests have been validated for the specific purpose for which they are used. 20 U.S.C. § 1414(b)(3)(B)(I).

109. No administrative remedy exists under IDEA to address the wholesale denial of fundamental and federally mandated accommodations by the STATE BOARD OF EDUCATION. Accordingly, Plaintiffs are not required to exhaust the administrative procedures set forth in IDEA.

110. WHEREFORE, Plaintiffs request relief as set forth below.

FOURTH CLAIM

VIOLATION OF DUE PROCESS CLAUSE OF CONSTITUTION

111. Plaintiffs incorporate by reference the allegations in paragraphs 1 through 110 inclusive.

112. The actions of Defendants have violated and continue to violate the Fourteenth Amendment to the United States Constitution in that Defendants have failed to provide Plaintiff children and their parents

with adequate notice of the testing requirements and of the severe consequences of failing to pass the tests and achieve a Certificate of Initial Mastery. Due to the lack of adequate notice, parents and educators have not had sufficient time to consider and determine whether and how the skills tested on the statewide tests should become part of a child's IEP or Section 504 Plan.

113. Defendants have violated and continue to violate the Fourteenth Amendment to the United States Constitution by failing to create and implement clear, consistent and understandable policies and procedures regarding provision of reasonable accommodations on the statewide tests. As a result, parents have been unable to make informed choices regarding their child's education and have, in many cases, been misled to believe that their child will be allowed to take the statewide assessments with accommodations.

114. Defendants have violated and continue to violate the Fourteenth Amendment to the United States Constitution by failing to establish a procedure for parents and children to challenge even the most arbitrary conduct with regard to the denials of reasonable accommodations on the CIM screening tests.

115. The actions of Defendants have violated and continue to violate the Fourteenth Amendment to the United States Constitution because the statewide screening tests, as currently formulated and administered, lack both instructional and curricular validity. The Oregon schools have never taught or trained children with learning disabilities many of the skills currently being tested on the statewide screening tests. Instead, Defendants have embarked upon a test-first-provide-education-later procedure, which effectively makes it impossible for children with learning disabilities to pass the required exams.

116. The actions of Defendants have violated and continue to violate the Fourteenth Amendment to the United States Constitution in that the statewide screening tests are fundamentally unfair because they test students on their disabilities.

117. WHEREFORE, Plaintiffs request relief as set forth below.

FIFTH CLAIM

VIOLATION OF OREGON CONSTITUTION—DUE PROCESS

118. Plaintiffs incorporate by reference herein the allegations in paragraphs 1 through 117 inclusive.

119. Article I, Section 10 of the Oregon Constitution guarantees due process of law to all citizens of the State of Oregon.

120. Plaintiffs are citizens of the State of Oregon.

121. The actions of Defendants have violated and continue to violate the due process protections of the Oregon Constitution in that Defendants have failed to provide Plaintiff children and their parents with adequate notice of the testing requirements and of the severe consequences of failing to pass the tests and achieve a Certificate of Initial Mastery. Due to the lack of adequate notice, parents and educators have not had sufficient time to consider and determine whether and how the skills tested on the statewide tests should become part of a child's IEP or Section 504 Plan.

122. Defendants have violated and continue to violate the due process protections of the Oregon Constitution by failing to create and implement clear, consistent and understandable policies and procedures regarding provision of reasonable accommodations on the statewide tests. As a result, parents have been unable to make informed choices regarding their child's education and have, in many cases, been misled to believe that their child will be allowed to take the statewide assessments with accommodations.

123. The actions of Defendants have violated and continue to violate the due process protections of the Oregon Constitution because the statewide screening tests, as currently formulated and administered, lack curricular validity. The Oregon schools have never taught or trained children with learning disabilities many of the skills currently being tested on the statewide screening tests. Instead, Defendants have embarked upon a test-first-provide-education-later procedure, which effectively makes it impossible for children with learning disabilities to pass the required exams.

124. The actions of Defendants have violated and continue to violate the due process protections of the Oregon Constitution in that the statewide screening tests are fundamentally unfair because they test students on their disabilities.

125. WHEREFORE, Plaintiffs request relief as set forth below.

SIXTH CLAIM

VIOLATION OF O.R.S. § 343

126. Plaintiffs incorporate by reference herein the allegations in paragraphs 1 through 125 inclusive.

127. By implementing an across the board policy prohibiting the use of certain accommodations on the statewide screening tests, Defendants have violated Oregon law which requires that each school district shall make assistive technology devices or assistive technology services, or both, available to a child with a disability if required as part of a

child's special education, related services or supplementary aids and services. O.R.S. § 343.223.

128. WHEREFORE, Plaintiffs request relief as set forth below.

SEVENTH CLAIM

VIOLATION OF O.R.S. § 659

129. Plaintiffs incorporate by reference herein the allegations in paragraphs 1 through 128 inclusive.

130. By subjecting Plaintiff children to discrimination on the basis of disability, Defendants have violated O.R.S. § 659.150.

131. WHEREFORE, Plaintiffs request relief as set forth below.

EIGHTH CLAIM

DECLARATORY RELIEF

132. Plaintiffs incorporate by reference herein the allegations in paragraphs 1 through 131 inclusive.

133. Plaintiffs contend, and are informed and believe that Defendants deny that the STATE BOARD has failed to comply with applicable law prohibiting discrimination against persons with disabilities and is in violation of the Americans with Disabilities Act, 42 U.S.C. § 12101, *et seq.*; Section 504 of the Rehabilitation Act of 1973, 29 U.S.C. § 794, *et seq.*; the United States Constitution; the Oregon State Constitution; Oregon Laws; and 42 U.S.C. § 1983 based upon violations of the Individuals with Disabilities Education Act, 20 U.S.C. § 1400, *et seq.*

134. A judicial declaration is necessary and appropriate at this time in order that each of the parties may know his or her respective rights and duties and act accordingly.

135. WHEREFORE, Plaintiffs request relief as set forth below.

RELIEF REQUESTED

WHEREFORE, Plaintiffs pray for relief as follows:

136. An order and judgment enjoining Defendants from violating 42 U.S.C. § 1983 based upon violations of the Individuals with Disabilities Education Act; the Americans with Disabilities Act; the Rehabilitation Act of 1973; the United States Constitution; the Oregon Constitution; Oregon Revised Statutes § 343; and Oregon Revised Statutes § 659.

137. A declaration that the Defendants have discriminated against Plaintiffs, who are children with disabilities in violation of the Individuals with Disabilities Education Act; the Americans with Disabilities

Act; the Rehabilitation Act of 1973; the United States Constitution; the Oregon Constitution; Oregon Revised Statutes § 343; and Oregon Revised Statutes § 659.

138. General and special damages for the named Plaintiffs according to proof at trial;

139. Plaintiffs' reasonable attorney fees and costs; and

140. Such other and further relief as the Court deems just and proper.

RESPECTFULLY SUBMITTED,

DATE: _____, 1999

By: SID WOLINSKY
California State Bar No. 33716
Telephone: (510) 451-8644
Attorney for Plaintiffs

By: JEFFREY P. FOOTE
Oregon State Bar No. 74098
Telephone: (503) 228-1133
Attorney for Plaintiffs

JURY TRIAL DEMANDED

Plaintiffs hereby demand a trial by jury.

DATE: _____, 1999

By: SID WOLINSKY
California State Bar No. 33716
Telephone: (510) 451-8644
Attorney for Plaintiffs

By: JEFFREY P. FOOTE
Oregon State Bar No. 74098
Telephone: (503) 228-1133
Attorney for Plaintiffs

APPENDIX 8:
SELECTED PROVISIONS OF THE AMERICANS WITH DISABILITIES ACT OF 1990

TITLE II—PUBLIC SERVICES

Subtitle A. Prohibition Against Discrimination and Other Generally Applicable Provisions

Section 12131. Definitions

As used in this subchapter:

(1) Public entity—The term "public entity" means—

(A) any State or local government;

(B) any department, agency, special purpose district, or other instrumentality of a State or States or local government; and

(C) the National Railroad Passenger Corporation, and any commuter authority (as defined in section 24102(4) of title 49).

(2) Qualified individual with a disability—The term "qualified individual with a disability" means an individual with a disability who, with or without reasonable modifications to rules, policies, or practices, the removal of architectural, communication, or transportation barriers, or the provision of auxiliary aids and services, meets the essential eligibility requirements for the receipt of services or the participation in programs or activities provided by a public entity.

Section 12132. Discrimination

Subject to the provisions of this subchapter, no qualified individual with a disability shall, by reason of such disability, be excluded from participation in or be denied the benefits of the services, programs, or activities of a public entity, or be subjected to discrimination by any such entity.

Section 12133. Enforcement

The remedies, procedures, and rights set forth in section 794a of title 29 shall be the remedies, procedures, and rights this subchapter provides to any person alleging discrimination on the basis of disability in violation of section 12132 of this title.

Section 12134. Regulations

(a) In general

Not later than 1 year after July 26, 1990, the Attorney General shall promulgate regulations in an accessible format that implement this part. Such regulations shall not include any matter within the scope of the authority of the Secretary of Transportation under section 12143, 12149, or 12164 of this title.

(b) Relationship to other regulations

Except for "program accessibility, existing facilities", and "communications", regulations under subsection (a) of this section shall be consistent with this chapter and with the coordination regulations under part 41 of title 28, Code of Federal Regulations (as promulgated by the Department of Health, Education, and Welfare on January 13, 1978), applicable to recipients of Federal financial assistance under section 794 of title 29. With respect to "program accessibility, existing facilities", and "communications", such regulations shall be consistent with regulations and analysis as in part 39 of title 28 of the Code of Federal Regulations, applicable to federally conducted activities under section 794 of title 29.

(c) Standards

Regulations under subsection (a) of this section shall include standards applicable to facilities and vehicles covered by this part, other than facilities, stations, rail passenger cars, and vehicles covered by part B of this subchapter. Such standards shall be consistent with the minimum guidelines and requirements issued by the Architectural and Transportation Barriers Compliance Board in accordance with section 12204(a) of this title.

SECTION 502. STATE IMMUNITY

A State shall not be immune under the eleventh amendment to the Constitution of the United States from an action in Federal or State court of competent jurisdiction for a violation of this Act. In any action against a State for a violation of the requirements of this Act, remedies (including remedies both at law and in equity) are available for such a violation to the same extent as such remedies are available for such a violation in an action against any public or private entity other than a State.

SECTION 503. PROHIBITION AGAINST RETALIATION AND COERCION

(a) Retaliation. No person shall discriminate against any individual because such individual has opposed any act or practice made unlawful by this Act or because such individual made a charge, testified, assisted, or participated in any manner in an investigation, proceeding, or hearing under this Act.

(b) Interference, Coercion, or Intimidation. It shall be unlawful to coerce, intimidate, threaten, or interfere with any individual in the exercise or enjoyment of, or on account of his or her having exercised or enjoyed, or on account of his or her having aided or encouraged any other individual in the exercise or enjoyment of, any right granted or protected by this Act.

(c) Remedies and Procedures. The remedies and procedures available under sections 107, 203, and 308 of this Act shall be available to aggrieved persons for violations of subsections (a) and (b), with respect to title I, title II and title III, respectively.

SECTION 505. ATTORNEYS FEES

In any action or administrative proceeding commenced pursuant to this Act, the court or agency, in its discretion, may allow the prevailing party, other than the United States, a reasonable attorneys fee, including litigation expenses, and costs, and the United States shall be liable for the foregoing the same as a private individual.

APPENDIX 9:
DIRECTORY OF UNITED STATES DEPARTMENT OF EDUCATION
REGIONAL OFFICES

REGION	AREAS COVERED	ADDRESS	TELEPHONE	FAX
REGION I	CT, MA, ME, NH, RI, VT	U.S. Department of Education 540 McCormack Courthouse Boston, MA 02109-4557	(617) 223-9317	(617) 223-9324
REGION II	NJ, NY, PR, VI	U.S. Department of Education 26 Federal Plaza, Room 36-120 New York, NY 10278-0195	(212) 264-7005	(212) 264-4427
REGION III	DC, DE, MD, PA, VA, WV	U.S. Department of Education 3535 Market Street, Room 16350 Philadelphia, PA 19104	(215) 596-1001	(215) 596-1094
REGION IV	AL, FL, GA, KY, MS, NC, SC, TN	U.S. Department of Education P.O. Box 1777 101 Marietta Tower Bldg, Suite 2221 Atlanta, GA 30323	(404) 331-2502	(404) 331-5382

REGION	AREAS COVERED	ADDRESS	TELEPHONE	FAX
REGION V	IL, IN, MI, MN, OH, WI	U.S. Department of Education 401 South State Street, Suite 700A Chicago, IL 60605-1225	(312) 353-5215	(312) 353-5147
REGION VI	AR, LA, NM, OK, TX	U.S. Department of Education 1200 Main Tower Bldg, Room 2125 Dallas, TX, 75202	(214) 767-3626	(214) 767-3634
REGION VII	IA, KS, MO, NE	U.S. Department of Education 10220 North Executive Hills Blvd. 9th Floor Kansas City, MO 64153-1367	(816) 891-7972	(816) 374-6442
REGION VIII	CO, MT, ND, SD, UT, WY	U.S. Department of Education Federal Building 1244 Speer Blvd, Suite 310 Denver, CO 80204-3582	(303) 844-3544	(303) 844-2524
REGION IX	AS, AZ, CA, HI, CN, MI, GU	U.S. Department of Education 50 United Nations Plaza, Room 205 San Francisco, CA 94102	(415) 556-4920	(415) 556-7242
REGION X	AK, ID, OR, WA	U.S. Department of Education Jackson Federal Building 915 2nd Avenue, Room 3362 Seattle, WA 98174-1099	(206) 220-7800	(206) 220-7806

APPENDIX 10:
DIRECTORY OF UNITED STATES EDUCATION DEPARTMENT REGIONAL EDUCATIONAL LABORATORIES

REGION	AREAS COVERED	NAME	ADDRESS	TELEPHONE	FAX	SPECIALTY AREA
Appalachian Region	KY, TN, VA, WV	Appalachia Educational Laboratory, Inc. (AEL)	1031 Quarrier Street PO Box 1348 Charleston, WV 25325	(304) 347-0400	(304) 347-0487	Rural Education
Western Region	AZ, CA, NV, UT	WestEd	730 Harrison Street San Francisco, CA 94107	(415) 565-3000	(415) 565-3012	Assessment and Accountability

REGION	AREAS COVERED	NAME	ADDRESS	TELEPHONE	FAX	SPECIALTY AREA
Central Region	CO, KS, MO, NE, ND, SD, WY	Mid-continent Regional Educational Laboratory (McREL)	2550 S Parker Road Suite 500 Aurora, CO 80014	(303) 337-0990	(303) 337-3005	Curriculum, Learning and Instruction
Midwestern Region	IA, IL, IN, MI, MN, OH, WI	North Central Regional Educational Laboratory (NCREL)	1900 Spring Road Suite 300 Oak Brook, IL 60521	(630) 571-4700	(630) 571-4716	Technology
Northwestern Region	AK, ID, MT, OR, WA	Northwest Regional Educational Laboratory (NWREL)	101 SW Main Street Suite 500 Portland, OR 97204	(503) 275-9500	(503) 275-9489	School Change Processes

REGION	AREAS COVERED	NAME	ADDRESS	TELEPHONE	FAX	SPECIALTY AREA
Pacific Region	American Samoa, Commonwealth of the Northern Mariana Islands, Federated States of Micronesia, Guam, Hawaii, Republic of the Marshall Islands, Republic of Paleu	Pacific Resources for Education & Learning (PREL)l	828 Fort Street Mall Suite 500 Honolulu, HI 96813	(808) 533-6000	(808) 533-7599	Language and Cultural Diversity
Northeastern Region	CT, MA, ME, NH, NY, PR, RI, VI, VT	Lab at Brown University Education Alliance (LAB)	222 Richmond St. Suite 300 Providence, Rhode Island 02903	(401) 274-9548	(401) 421-7650	Language and Cultural Diversity
Mid-Atlantic Region	DC, DE, MD, NJ, PA	The Laboratory for Student Success (LSS)	933 Ritter Annex 13th and Cecil B. Moore Philadelphia, PA 19122	(215) 204-3001	none	Urban Education

REGION	AREAS COVERED	NAME	ADDRESS	TELEPHONE	FAX	SPECIALTY AREA
Southeastern Region	AL, FL, GA, MS, NC, SC	South Eastern Regional Vision for Education (SERVE)	PO Box 5367 Greensboro, NC 27435	(910) 334-3211	(910) 334-3268	Early Childhood Education
Southwestern Region	AR, LA, NM, OK, TX	Southwest Educational Development Laboratory (SEDL)	211 East Seventh Street Austin, TX 78701	(512) 476-6861	(512) 476-2286	Language and Cultural Diversity

Source: U.S. Education Department.

APPENDIX 11:

DIRECTORY OF UNITED STATES EDUCATION DEPARTMENT NATIONAL RESEARCH AND DEVELOPMENT CENTERS

NAME	ADDRESS	TELEPHONE	E-MAIL
Center for Research on Education, Diversity and Excellence (CREDE)	University of California Santa Cruz 1156 High Street Santa Cruz, CA 95064	(408) 459-3500	http://www.crede.ucsc.edu
Center for Research on the Education of Students Placed At-Risk (CRESPAR)	Johns Hopkins University CSOS 3505 North Charles Street Baltimore, MD 21218	(410) 516-8800	http://scov.csos.jhu.edu/crespar/ CReSPaR.html
CALIFORNIA, Center for Research on Evaluation, Standards, and Student Testing (CRESST), University of California Los Angeles,	Graduate School of Education 1339 Moore Hall 405 Hilgard Avenue Los Angeles, CA 90024	(310) 206-1530	http://cresst96.cse.ucla.edu

NAME	ADDRESS	TELEPHONE	E-MAIL
Center for the Improvement of Early Reading Achievement (CIERA)	University of Michigan School of Education 610 E. University Avenue, Rm 1600 Ann Arbor, MI 48109-1259	(734) 647-6940	http://www.ciera.org/
Center for the Study of Teaching and Policy (CTP)	University of Washington College of Education Box 353600 Seattle, Washington 98195	(206) 221-4114	http://www.educ.washington.edu/COE/center/StudyTeachPolCtr.htm
National Center for Early Development and Learning (NCEDL)	University of North Carolina Chapel Hill Frank Porter Graham Child Development Center CB #4100 Chapel Hill, NC 27599-4100	(919) 966-4250	http://www.fpg.unc.edu/ncedl/
National Center for Improving Student Learning and Achievement in Mathematics and Science, Wisconsin Center for Education Research School of Education	University of Wisconsin 1025 West Johnson Street Madison, WI 53706	(608) 263-4285	http://www.wcer.wisc.edu/NCISLA/
National Center for Postsecondary Improvement (NCPI)	CERAS 508, School of Education 520 Galvez Mall, Stanford University Stanford, CA 94305-3084	(650) 723-7724	

NAME	ADDRESS	TELEPHONE	E-MAIL
National Center for the Study of Adult Learning and Literacy (NCSALL)	Harvard Graduate School of Education 101 Nichols House, Appian Way Cambridge, MA 02138	(617) 495-4843	http://hugse1.harvard.edu/~ncsall
National Center on Increasing the Effectiveness of State and Local Education Reform Efforts	Consortium for Policy Research in Education (CPRE) Graduate School of Education University of Pennsylvania 3440 Market Street, Suite 560 Philadelphia, PA 19104-3325	(215) 573-0700	http://www.upenn.edu/gse/cpre
National Research & Development Center on English Learning & Achievement (CELA)	University of Albany State University of New York School of Education 1400 Washington Avenue Albany, NY 12222	(518) 442-5026	http://www.albany.edu/cela/
National Research Center on the Gifted and Talented (NRC/GT)	University of Connecticut 362 Fairfield Road U-7 Storrs, CT 06269-2007	(860) 486-4676	http://www.ucc.uconn.edu/~wwwgt/nrcgt.html

APPENDIX 12:
DIRECTORY OF ATTORNEYS WHO REPRESENT PARENTS OF CHILDREN WITH DISABILITIES

STATE	FIRM	ADDRESS	TELEPHONE	FAX
ARIZONA	Jerri Katzerman Arizona Center for Disability Law	3839 N. Third St., #209 Phoenix, AZ 85012	602-274-6284	602-274-6779
CALIFORNIA	John M. Bayne, Jr. Sole Practitioner	12400 Wilshire Blvd., #400 Los Angeles, CA 90025-1023	310-390-3600	310-572-0673
CALIFORNIA	Thomas E. Beltran Sole Practitioner	137 orth Larchmont Blvd, #256 Los Angeles, CA 90004	213-467-0702	818-891-5070
CALIFORNIA	Allison B. Brightman/Donna R. Levin Brightman & Levin	1125 Lindero Canyon Rd., #A8 Westlake Village, CA 91362	818-889-898	818-889-8689

STATE	FIRM	ADDRESS	TELEPHONE	FAX
CALIFORNIA	Michael S. Cochrane Sole Practitioner	12315 Oak Knoll Rd., #110 Poway, CA 92064	858-486-3699	858-486-3299
CALIFORNIA	Rene Thomas Folse Miller and Folse	101 Moody Ct. Thousand Oaks, CA 91361	805-497-0857	805-495-2684
CALIFORNIA	Eric B. Freedus Frank and Freedus	APC 1202 Kettner Blvd., #6000 San Diego, CA 92101	619-239-3000	619-236-0217
CALIFORNIA	Rich Kitchens Sole Practitioner	4418 Water Oak Court Concord, CA 94521	925-687-0143	925-687-0143
CALIFORNIA	Nancy J. LoDolce Sole Practitioner	411 Russell Ave. Santa Rosa, CA 95403	707-544-4600	N/A
CALIFORNIA	Kathleen M. Loyer Sole Practitioner	940 Calle Amanecer, Suite L San Clemente, CA 92673	949-369-1082	949-498-2958
CALIFORNIA	Gary F. Redenbacher Sole Practitioner	5610 Scotts Valley Drive, #35 Santa Cruz, CA 95066	831-439-8821	831-438-3121
CALIFORNIA	Jane F. Reid Sole Practitioner,	121A North Main Street Sebastopol, CA 95472	707-824-1466	707-874-2718
CALIFORNIA	Scott C. Van Soye Sole Practitioner	1920 E. 17th St. Santa Ana, CA 92705-8626	714-835-3090	714-571-3993
CALIFORNIA	Valerie Vanaman Newman, Aaronson, & Vanaman	14001 Ventura Blvd. Sherman Oaks, CA 91423-3558	818-990-7722	818-501-1306
CALIFORNIA	Bob N. Varma/Geralyn M. Clancy Varma & Clancy	910 Florin Rd., #212 Sacramento, CA 95831	916-429-4080	916-429-4085

STATE	FIRM	ADDRESS	TELEPHONE	FAX
COLORADO	Bradley M. Bittan Law Office of Bradley M. Bittan	10940 South Parker Rd., #473 Parker, CO 80134	303-805-3543	303-841-1659
COLORADO	Jack D. Robinson Spies, Powers & Robinson	1660 Lincoln St., #2220 Denver, CO 80264	303-830-7090	303-830-7089
COLORADO	Susan M. Weiner Law Office of Susan M. Weiner	4450 Arapahoe Ave., #100 Boulder, CO 80303	303-415-2564	303-444-1038
CONNECTICUT	Lawrence D. Church Sole Practitioner	120 East Ave. Norwalk, CT 06852	203-853-4999	203-853-9429
CONNECTICUT	Howard Klebanoff Howard Klebanoff, P.C.	433 South Main St., #102 West Hartford, CT 06110	860-313-5005	860-313-5010
CONNECTICUT	Ann A. Nevel Sole Practitioner	161 Paper Mill Rd. New Milford, CT 06776	860-354-6780	860-355-7144
CONNECTICUT	Winona W. Zimberlin Sole Practitioner	2 Congress St. Hartford, CT 06114-1024	860-249-5291	860-247-4194
DISTRICT OF COLUMBIA	Beth Goodman Feldesman, Tucke, Leifer, Fidell & Bank	2001 L St., N.W., 3d Flr. Washington, DC 20036-4910	202-466-8960	202-293-8103
DISTRICT OF COLUMBIA	Margaret A. Kohn Kohn & Einstein	1320 19th St., N.W., #200 Washington, DC 20036	202-667-2330	202-667-2302
DISTRICT OF COLUMBIA	James R. Marsh/Sara Dorsch The Children's Law CenterInc.	717 D St., N.W., #210 Washington, DC 20004-2807	202-783-9404	202-783-9403

STATE	FIRM	ADDRESS	TELEPHONE	FAX
DISTRICT OF COLUMBIA	Jerrold D. Miller Miller & Miller	1990 M St., N.W., #760 Washington, DC 20036	202-785-2720	202-775-8519
DISTRICT OF COLUMBIA	Travis A. Murrel Murrell & Brown	1401 I St., N.W., #250 Washington, DC 20005	202-289-9001	202-290-9094
FLORIDA	S. James Rosenfeld The EDLAW Center	P.O. Box 81-7327 Hollywood, FL 33081-0327	954-966-4489	561-373-0885
FLORIDA	Joseph Nathaniel Baron Law Office of J.N. Baron, P.A.	P.O. Drawer 1088 Lakeland, FL 33802-1088	941-687-1755	941-687-389
FLORIDA	Michael L. Boswell Michael L. Boswell, P.A.	1009 East Highway 436 Altamonte Springs, FL 32701	407-831-1231	407-831-5813
FLORIDA	Eric Hightower Davis, Gordon & Doner, P.A.	515 N. Flagler Dr., #700 West Palm Beach, FL 33401	561-659-7337	561-659-0143
FLORIDA	Mark S. Kamleiter Sole Practitioner	600 First Ave. N., #206 St. Petersburg, FL 33701-3609	813-824-8989	813-824-6389
FLORIDA	Doris Landis Raskin Sole Practitioner	P.O. Box 1667 Stuart, FL 34995	561-221-2173	561-221-3561
FLORIDA	Joshua H. Rosen Joshua H. Rosen, Chartered	4370 S. Tamiami Trail, #324 Sarasota, FL 34231	941-921-7111	941-927-6616
FLORIDA	Leslie C. Scott Sheppard, White and Thomas, P.A.	215 Washington St. Jacksonville, FL 32202	904-356-9661	904-356-9667

STATE	FIRM	ADDRESS	TELEPHONE	FAX
GEORGIA	Dawn R. Smith Zimring, Smith & Billips, P.C.	615 Peachtree St., N.E., #1100 Atlanta, GA 30308	404-607-1600	404-607-1355
GEORGIA	Torin D. Togut Georgia Legal Services Program,	1100 Spring St., #200-A Atlanta, GA 30309-2848	404-206-5175	404-206-5346
HAWAII	Shelby Anne Floyd Alston, Hunt, Floyd & Ing	1001 Bishop St., 18th Flr. Honolulu, HI 96813	808-524-1800	808-524-4591
HAWAII	Keith H.S. Peck Peck & Associate	1511 Nuuanu Ave., PH #3 Honolulu, HI 96817	808-545-7595	N/A
HAWAII	Arnold T. Phillips II Phillips, Kinkley & Cox	1001 Bishop St., #1250 Honolulu, HI 96813	808-521-8770	808-521-9715
ILLINOIS	Margie Best Law Offices of Margie Best	One North LaSalle St., #2200 Chicago, IL 60602	312-263-4040	312-263-1022
ILLINOIS	Barry D. Bright Sole Practitioner	P.O. Box 603 Flora, IL 62839	618-662-9585	618-662-7220
ILLINOIS	Matthew Cohen Monahan & Cohen	225 West Washington, #2300 Chicago, IL 60606	312-419-0252	312-419-7428
ILLINOIS	John W. Gaffney Weisz & Michling	2030 North Seminary Ave. Woodstock, IL 60098	815-338-3838	815-338-7817
ILLINOIS	Deborah W. Owens Sole Practitioner	120 E. Ogden Ave., Ste. 8 Hinsdale, IL 60521	630-789-5856	630-789-9503
ILLINOIS	Miriam F. Solo Sole Practitioner	6334 N. Whipple, #2B Chicago, IL 60659	773-973-3143	773-465-5821

STATE	FIRM	ADDRESS	TELEPHONE	FAX
IOWA	Iowa P & A Iowa P & A	3015 Merle Hay Rd., #6 Des Moines, IA 50310	515-278-2502	515-278-0539
KANSAS	Dwight A. Corrin Sole Practitioner	P.O. Box 47828 Wichita, KS 67201-7828	316-263-9706	316-263-6385
KANSAS	Peter John Orsi Law Office of Peter John Orsi	610 North Tyler Rd. Wichita, KS 67212	316-729-8825	316-729-8771
KANSAS	Alan R. Post Sole Practitioner	1803 N. Siefkin St. Wichita, KS 67208-1758	316-686-8232	316-686-8248
KENTUCKY	C. David Emerson/Robert C. Welleford Emerson & Associates	501 Darby Creek, Unit 41 Lexington, KY 40509	606-264-1664	606-264-1670
MAINE	Richard L. O'Meara Murray, Plumb & Murray	75 Pearl St. Portland, ME 04104-5085	207-773-5651	207-773-8023
MARYLAND	Jeanne Asherman Law Offices of J. Asherman	9015 Walden Rd. Silver Spring, MD 20901	301-587-6990	301-587-6680
MARYLAND	Philip A. Guzman Sole Practitioner	The Metropolitan Bldg. 8720 Georgia Ave., #706 Silver Spring, MD 20910	301-587-5285	301-565-9391
MARYLAND	Patrick J. Hoover Patrick J. Hoover Law Offices	600 Jefferson Plaza. #308 Rockville, MD 20852	301-424-5777	301-217-9297
MARYLAND	Beth A. Jackson Sole Practitioner	3454 Ellicott Center Drive, #203 Ellicott City, MD 21043	410-465-8904	410-465-0168
MARYLAND	Mark B. Martin Sole Practitioner	207 E. Redwood St., #703 Baltimore, MD 21202	410-779-7770	410-576-9391

STATE	FIRM	ADDRESS	TELEPHONE	FAX
MARYLAND	Walter D. McQuie Sole Practitioner	346 Glebe Rd. Easton, MD 21601	410-820-6441	410-763-9312
MARYLAND	Robert H. Plotkin Law Office of Robert H. Plotkin	113 North Washington St., #320 Rockville, MD 20850	301-279-7387	301-279-0386
MARYLAND	Laura N. Venezia Sole Practitioner	1317 Orchard Way Frederick, MD 21703	301-694-5530	N/A
MASSACHUSETTS	Glenn Everett Churchill Churchill Law Associates	189 Flagler Drive Marshfield, MA 02050-2842	781-837-2183	781-834-2061
MASSACHUSETTS	Heather Gold Eckert, Seamans, Cherin & Mellot, LLC	One International Place 18th Flr. Boston, MA 02110	617-342-6800	617-342-6899
MASSACHUSETTS	Robert K. Crabtree/Lawrence Kotin/Richard Howard/Eileen Hagerty Kotin, Crabtree & Strong, LLP	One Bowdoin Square Boston, MA 02114-2919	617-227-7031	617-367-2988
MASSACHUSETTS	Kenneth J. Gogel Gogel Law Office	34 Depot St. Pittsfield, MA 01201	413-442-8803	413-443-3461
MASSACHUSETTS	E. Alexandra Golden Sole Practitioner	175 Highland Ave. Needham, MA 02494	781-433-8665	781-444-8706
MASSACHUSETTS	Carol E. Kervick Sole Practitioner	21 Concord St. Charlestown, MA 02129	617-242-3458	617-242-3458

STATE	FIRM	ADDRESS	TELEPHONE	FAX
MASSACHUSETTS	John-Paul LaPre Law Offices of John-Paul LaPre	111 Lakeside Ave. Marlborough, MA 01752	508-481-5505	508-481-4415
MASSACHUSETTS	Geraldine ten Brinke Sole Practitioner	10 Concord Rd. Sudbury, MA 01776	978-443-9005	978-443-0543
MICHIGAN	John F. Brower Law Office of John F. Brower	121 West North St., #5 Brighton, MI 48116	810-227-9797	810-227-7996
MICHIGAN	Richard J. Landau Dykema Gossett, PLLC	315 E. Eisenhower Pkwy., #100 Ann Arbor, MI 48108	734-214-7669	734-214-7696
MICHIGAN	Don L. Rosenberg Barron & Rosenberg, P.C.	200 East Long Lake Rd., #180 Bloomfield Hills, MI 48304-2361	248-647-4440	248-647-4727
MICHIGAN	Annette E. Skinner Sole Practitioner	509 E. Grand River Ave., Suite A Lansing, MI 48906	517-484-7820	517-474-7824
MINNESOTA	Thomas B. James Sole Practitioner	440 N. Broadway Ave. Cokato, MN 55321	320-286-6425	320-286-6425
MINNESOTA	Sonja D. Kerr Kerr Law Offices	5972 Cahill Ave., #110 Inver Grove Heights, MN 55076	651-552-4900	651-552-4942
NEVADA	Thomas J. Moore Sole Practitioner	2810 W. Charleston Blvd., #F-62 Las Vegas, NV 89102	702-593-9556	702-870-1029
NEW JERSEY	Penelope A. Boyd Law Offices of Penelope A. Boyd	3000 Atrium Way, #292 Mt. Laurel, NJ 08054	609-273-3142	609-273-6913
NEW JERSEY	John M. Capasso Sole Practitioner	1230 Shore Rd. Linwood, NJ 08221	609-926-9288	609-926-2288

STATE	FIRM	ADDRESS	TELEPHONE	FAX
NEW JERSEY	Jamie Epstein Sole Practitioner	38 West End Ave. Haddonfield, NJ 08033	609-354-8008	609-354-8008
NEW JERSEY	Carole Ann Geronimo Sole Practitioner	1 DeMercurio Drive Allendale, NJ 07401	201-512-4400	201-512-4403
NEW JERSEY	Herbert D. Hinkle/Linda R. Robinson Law Offices of Herbert D. Hinkle	2651 Main St., #A Lawrenceville, NJ 08648	609-896-4200	609-895-9524
NEW JERSEY	George M. Holland Williams, Caliri, Miller & Otley	1428 Route 23 Wayne, NJ 07474	201-694-0800	201-694-0302
NEW JERSEY	Harriet W. Rothfeld Sole Practitioner	225 Millburn Ave., #206 Millburn, NJ 07041-1712	201-376-7373	201-376-3847
NEW JERSEY	Philip D. Stern Sole Practitioner	225 Millburn Ave., #208 Millburn, NJ 07041-1712	201-912-9393	201-912-4343
NEW JERSEY	Theodore A. Sussan/Staci J. Greenwald Sussan and Greenwald	407 Main St. Spotswood, NJ 08884	732-251-8585	732-238-0900
NEW YORK	Charles G. Davis, Esq. Davis and Davis	20 Squadron Blvd., #350 New City, NY	914-634-6633	914-634-7688
NEW YORK	Michael E. Deffet Leon & Deffet	235 Brooksite Drive Hauppauge, NY 11788	516-360-6694	516-361-7324
NEW YORK	Barbara J. Ebenstein Ebenstein & Ebenstein	801 Second Ave., #1402 New York, NY 10017	212-687-4433	212-687-4436

STATE	FIRM	ADDRESS	TELEPHONE	FAX
NEW YORK	Sami Kahn Sole Practitioner	305 Broadway, #500 New York, NY 10007	212-577-6877	N/A
NEW YORK	Deborah R. Monheit Sole Practitioner	P.O. Box 163 East Setauket, N.Y. 11773	516-751-6070	516-651-6512
NEW YORK	Neal H. Rosenberg Law Offices of Neal H. Rosenberg	9 Murray St., #7W New York, NY 10007-228	212-732-9450	212-732-4443
NEW YORK	Robert Testino Sole Practitioner	91 Columbia St. Albany, NY 12210	518-426-4667	518-462-3826
NORTH CAROLINA	Edward J. Bedford Pinna, Johnston, O'Donoghue & Burwell, P.A.	P.O. Box 31788 Raleigh, NC 27622	919-755-1317	919-782-0452
NORTH CAROLINA	Barbara Jackson Holt & York, LLP	P.O. Box 17105 Raleigh, NC 27619	919-420-7826	919-420-7830
OHIO	Franklin J. Hickman/Janet L. Lowder/Melody L. Harness Hickman & Lowder Co., LPA	1370 Ontario St., #1620 Cleveland, OH 44113-1743	216-861-0360	216-861-3113
OHIO	Lisa B. Avirov Sole Practitioner	8070 Beechmont Ave., #4 Cincinnati, OH 45255	513-474-4466	513-474-5800
OHIO	Michael E. Deffet Leon & Deffet	P.O. Box 458 Phillipsburg, OH 45354	937-884-5540	937-884-5540
OHIO	Ohio State Legal Services Association, N/A	861 North High St. Columbus, OH 43215	614-299-2114	614-299-6364

STATE	FIRM	ADDRESS	TELEPHONE	FAX
OHIO	Nessa G. Siegel Nessa G. Siegel Co. Inc.	4070 Mayfield Rd. Cleveland, OH 44121	216-291-1300	216-291-9622
OKLAHOMA	Moura A.J. Robertson McCormick, Schoenenberger & Robertson, P.A.	1441 South Carson Ave. Tulsa, OK 74119-3417	918-582-3655	918-582-3657
OKLAHOMA	Mary J. Rounds Mary J. Rounds, P.C.	406 South Boulder Ave., #400 Tulsa, OK 74103	918-592-1900	918-592-0928
OREGON	David A. Bahr Bahr & Stotter Law Offices	259 E. Fifth Ave., #200 Eugene, OR 97401	541-686-3277	541-686-2130
OREGON	Mary E. Broadhurst Mary E. Broadhurst, P.C.	P.O. Box 11377 Eugene, OR 97440	541-683-8530	541-687-9767
OREGON	Dana R. Taylor Hagen, Dye, Hirschy & DiLorenzo, P.C.	One S.W. Columbia St., #1900 Portland, OR 97258	503-222-1812	503-274-7979
PENNSYLVANIA	Penelope A. Boyd Law Offices of Penelope A. Boyd	101 Breesey Court 517 East Lancaster Ave. Downington, PA 19335	610-873-6939	610-518-0349
PENNSYLVANIA	Paul J. Drucker Law Offices Bernard M. Gross, P.C.	1500 Walnut St., 6th Flr. Philadelphia, PA 19102	215-561-3600	215-561-3000
PENNSYLVANIA	J. Lawrence Hajduk/Mary L. Hajduk/Mark A. Rowan/Leslie Crosco J. Lawrence Hajduk & Associates	5340 National Pike Markleysburg, PA 15459	412-329-1133	412-329-8959

STATE	FIRM	ADDRESS	TELEPHONE	FAX
PENNSYLVANIA	Herbert D. Hinkle Law Offices of Herbert D. Hinkle	2651 Main St., #A Lawrenceville, NJ 08648	215-860-2100	609-895-9524
PENNSYLVANIA	Yvonne M. Husic Nicholas & Foreman, P.C.	4409 North Front St. Harrisburg, PA 17110-1709	717-236-9391	717-236-6602
PENNSYLVANIA	Elizabeth Kapo Sole Practitioner	34 N. Fifth St. Allentown, PA 18101	610-770-7399	610-770-6909
PENNSYLVANIA	Vivian B. Narehood Gibbel, Kraybill & Hess	41 East Orange St. Lancaster, PA 17602	717-291-1700	717-291-5547
PENNSYLVANIA	Philip Matthew Stinson, Sr. Stinson Law Associates, P.C.	895 Glenbrook Ave. Bryn Mawr, PA 19010-7340	610-519-0390	610-519-0394
PUERTO RICO	Wilfredo A. Ruiz W. A. Ruiz Law Offices	#49 Hiram Gonzalez St. Bayamon, PR 00959	787-787-2122	787-787-2302
RHODE ISLAND	Melissa A. Korpacz Korpacz & Associates	13 Dickinson Ave., #3 North Providence, RI 02904	401-723-0069	N/A
RHODE ISLAND	Richard D. Pass Pass Law Associates	1445 Wampanoag Trail, #115 East Providence, RI 02915	401-433-1414	401-433-1692
SOUTH DAKOTA	Robert J. Kean/John A. Hamilton/Lynne A. Valenti South Dakota Advocacy Services	221 S. Central Ave. Pierre, SD 57501-2453	605-224-8294	605-224-5125
TEXAS	C. Michael Black Law Office of C. Michael Black	2444 Times Blvd., #222 Houston, TX 77005	713-522-5999	713-522-2625

STATE	FIRM	ADDRESS	TELEPHONE	FAX
TEXAS	Chris Jonas Sole Practitioner	3349 Jamaica Dr. Corpus Christi, TX 78418	361-937-1801	361-937-1802
TEXAS	David Aaron Piña Lopez, Piña & Urrutia	611 South Congress, #340 Austin, TX 78704	512-442-7299	512-326-3171
TEXAS	Advocacy, Inc.	7800 Shoal Creek Blvd., #142-S Austin, TX 78757-1024	512-454-4816	512-323-0902
UTAH	David G. Challed Challed Law Offices	254 West 400 South, #320 Salt Lake City, UT 84101	801-355-3500	801-359-6873
VIRGINIA	Frank M. Feibelman Hill, Rainey & Eliades	731 W. Broadway P.O. Box 1007 Hopewell, VA 23860-1007	804-541-1941	804-541-5602
VIRGINIA	Barbara S. Jenkins Jenkins & Hagy, PLC	401 Ridge St. Charlottesville, VA 22902	804-296-4998	804-296-9647
VIRGINIA	Lois N. Manes Sole Practitioner	P.O. Box 1675 Williamsburg, VA 23187	757-229-6224	757-220-8515 10
VIRGINIA	Peter W.D. Wright Sole Practitioner	P.O. Box 1008 Deltaville, VA 23043-1008	804-776-7008	N/A
WASHINGTON	Steven N. Bogdon Blair, Schaefer Hutchison & Wolfe LLP.	105 W. Evergreen Blvd. P.O. Box 1148 Vancouver, WA 98666-1148	360-693-5883	360-693-1777
WASHINGTON	William L.E. Dussaul Sole Practitioner	219 East Galer St. Seattle, WA 98102-3794	206-324-4300	206-324-3106
WASHINGTON	Larry A. Jones Sole Practitioner	2118 8th Ave. Seattle, WA 98121	206-405-3240	206-405-3243

STATE	FIRM	ADDRESS	TELEPHONE	FAX
WASHINGTON	Edward L. Lane Sole Practitioner	607 SW Grady Way #110 Renton, WA 98055	425-226-1418	425-226-1246
WASHINGTON	Mary E. McKnew Sole Practitioner	7840 Warbler Ct. SE Olympia, WA 98513	360-459-0554	360-459-0359
WEST VIRGINIA	William F. Byrne Byrne & Hedge	141 Walnut St. Morgantown, WV 26505	304-296-0123	304-296-0713
WEST VIRGINIA	Robert J. O'Brien Sole Practitioner	43 S. Florida St. Buckhannon, WV 26201	304-472-2456	304-472-2456

Source: EDLAW, Inc., (http://www.edlaw.net/attylist.html).

APPENDIX 13:
DIRECTORY OF PARENT TRAINING AND INFORMATION CENTERS

Funded Centers, by State

Alabama
Special Education Action Committee, Inc.

Mavis   Smith
600 Bel-Air Boulevard, Suite 210
P.O. 161274
Mobile   AL   36616-2274
    Phone | 251-478-1208 Voice & TDD |
       Fax | 251-473-7877 | **800**   1-800-222-7322 AL only
    E-mail   seacofmobile@seacpac.com
      Web   www.seacparentsassistancecenter.com
   Serving   Statewide

Alaska
PARENTS, Inc.

Sanja   Bolling
4743 E. Northern Lights Blvd.
Anchorage   AK   99508
    Phone | 907-337-7678 Voice; 907-337-7629 TDD |
       Fax | 907-337-7671 | **800**   1-800-478-7678 in AK
    E-mail   parents@parentsinc.org
      Web   www.parentsinc.org
   Serving   Statewide

Arizona
Raising Special Kids

Joyce   Millard-Hoie
2400 North Central Avenue, Suite 200
Phoenix   AZ   85004
    Phone | 602-242-4366 Voice & TDD |
       Fax | 602-242-4306 | **800**   1-800-237-3007 in AZ
    E-mail   info@raisingspecialkids.org
      Web   www.raisingspecialkids.org
   Serving   Central and Northern AZ

Arkansas
Arkansas Disability Coalition

Wanda   Stovall
1123 South University Avenue, Suite 225
Little Rock   AR   72204-1605
    Phone | 501-614-7020 Voice & TDD |
       Fax | 501-614-9082 | **800**   1-800-223-1330 AR only
    E-mail   adcwstovall@earthlink.net
      Web   www.adcpti.org
   Serving   Statewide

California
DREDF

Susan   Henderson
2212 Sixth Street
Berkeley   CA   94710
    Phone | 510-644-2555 (TDD available) |
       Fax | 510-841-8645 | **800**   1-800-466-4232
    E-mail   dredf@dredf.org
      Web   www.dredf.org
   Serving   Northern California
           With Parents Helping Parents of Santa Clara

California
Matrix Parent Network and Resource Center

Nora   Thompson
94 Galli Drive, Suite C
Novato   CA   94949
    Phone | 415-884-3535 |
       Fax | 415-884-3555 | **800**   1-800-578-2592
    E-mail   norat@matrixparents.org
      Web   www.matrixparents.org
   Serving   Northern California
           With Parents Helping Parents of Santa Clara

California
Parents Helping Parents of Santa Clara

Mary Ellen   Peterson
3041 Olcott St.
Santa Clara   CA   95054-3222
    Phone | 408-727-5775 Voice / 408-727-7655 TDD |
       Fax | 408-727-0182 | **800**
    E-mail   info@php.com
      Web   www.php.com
   Serving   Northern California

California
Team of Advocates for Special Kids (TASK)

Joan Tellefsen/   Marta Anchondo
100 West Cerritos Ave.
Anaheim   CA   92805
    Phone | 714-533-8275 |
       Fax | 714-533-2533 | **800**
    E-mail
      Web   Southern California
   Serving

Funded Centers, by State

Colorado
PEAK Parent Center, Inc.

Barbara　　　　　　Buswell
611 North Weber, Suite 200
Colorado Springs　CO　80903
Phone 719-531-9400 voice / 719-531-9403 TDD
Fax 719-531-9452　**800** 1-800-284-0251
E-mail info@peakparent.org
Web www.peakparent.org
Serving Statewide

Georgia
Parents Educating Parents and Professionals for All Children (PEPPAC)
Linda　　　　　　Shepard
8957 Highway 5, Suite B
Douglasville　GA　30134
Phone 770-577-7771
Fax 770-577-7774　**800** 1-800-322-7065
E-mail peppinc@peppinc.org
Web www.peppinc.org
Serving Statewide

Connecticut
CPAC

Nancy　　　　　　Prescott
338 Main Street
Niantic　CT　06357
Phone 860-739-3089 Voice & TDD
Fax 860-739-7460　**800** 1-800-445-2722 in CT
E-mail cpac@cpacinc.org
Web www.cpacinc.org
Serving Statewide

Hawaii
AWARE

Jennifer　　　　　　Schember-Lang
200 N. Vineyard Blvd., Suite 310
Honolulu　HI　96817
Phone 808-536-9684 (voice) / 808-536-2280 (Voice & TTY)
Fax 808-537-6780　**800** 1-800-533-9684
E-mail jschember-lang@ldahawaii.org
Web www.ldahawaii.org
Serving Statewide

Delaware
Parent Information Center of Delaware (PIC/DE)

Marie-Anne　　　　　　Aghazadian
5570 Kirkwood Highway
Wilmington　DE　19808-5002
Phone 302-999-7394
Fax 302-999-7637　**800** 1-888-547-4412
E-mail maghaz@picofdel.org
Web www.picofdel.org
Serving Statewide

Idaho
Idaho Parents Unlimited, Inc.

Evelyn　　　　　　Mason
600 North Curtis Road, Suite 100
Boise　ID　83706
Phone 208-342-5884 Voice & TDD
Fax 208-342-1408　**800** 1-800-242-4785
E-mail parents@ipulidaho.org
Web www.ipulidaho.org
Serving Statewide

Florida
Family Network on Disabilities of Florida, Inc.

Millie Pou　　　　Nancy Gonsalves
2735 Whitney Road
Clearwater　FL　33760-1610
Phone 727-523-1130
Fax 727-523-8687　**800** 800-825-5736 FL only
E-mail fnd@fndfl.org
Web www.fndfl.org
Serving Statewide

Illinois
Family Resource Center on Disabilities

Charlotte　　　　　　Des Jardins
20 E. Jackson Blvd., Room 300
Chicago　IL　60604
Phone 312-939-3513 voice / 312-939-3519 TTY & TDY
Fax 312-939-7297　**800** 1-800-952-4199 IL only
E-mail frcdptifl@ameritech.net
Web www.frcd.org
Serving Statewide

Funded Centers, by State

Illinois
Designs for Change

Donald   Moore
29 East Madison, Suite 950
Chicago IL 60602
Phone 312-236-7252 voice / 312-857-1013 TDD
Fax 312-236-7927   **800**
E-mail markse@designsforchange.org
Web www.designsforchange.org
Serving Statewide

Indiana
IN*SOURCE

Richard   Burden
809 N. Michigan St.
South Bend IN 46601-1036
Phone 574-234-7101; 219-239-7275 TTD
Fax 574-234-7279   **800** 1-800-332-4433 in IN
E-mail insource@insource.org
Web www.insource.org
Serving Statewide

Iowa
Access for Special Kids (ASK)

Jule   Reynolds
321 East 6th Street
Des Moines IA 50309
Phone 515-243-1713
Fax 515-243-1902   **800** 1-800-450-8667
E-mail jule@askresource.org
Web www.askresource.org
Serving Statewide

Kansas
Families Together, Inc.

Connie   Zienkewicz
3033 West Second, Suite 106
Wichita KS 67203
Phone 316-945-7747
Fax 316-945-7795   **800** 1-888-815-6364
E-mail connie@familiestogetherinc.org
Web www.familiestogetherinc.com
Serving Statewide

Kentucky
KY Special Parent Involvement Network (KY-SPIN)

Paulette   Logsdon
10301 B Deering Road
Louisville KY 40272
Phone 502-937-6894
Fax 502-937-6464   **800** 1-800-525-7746
E-mail spininc@kyspin.com
Web www.kyspin.com
Serving Statewide

Louisiana
Project PROMPT

Cindy   Arceneaux
4323 Division Street, Suite 110
Metairie LA 70002-3179
Phone 504-888-9111
Fax 504-888-0246   **800** 1-800-766-7736
E-mail carceneaux@projectpromt.com
Web www.projectprompt.com
Serving Statewide

Maine
Maine Parent Federation

Janice   LaChance
PO Box 2067
Augusta ME 04338-2067
Phone 207-623-2144
Fax 207-623-2148   **800** 1-800-870-7746
E-mail parentconnect@mpf.org
Web www.mpf.org
Serving Statewide

Maryland
Parents Place of Maryland, Inc.

Josie   Thomas
7484 Candlewood Rd Suite S
Hanover MD 21076-1306
Phone 410-859-5300 Voice & TDD
Fax 410-859-5301   **800**
E-mail info@ppmd.org
Web www.ppmd.org
Serving Statewide

Funded Centers, by State

Massachusetts
Federation for Children with Special Needs

Richard   Robison
1135 Tremont Street, Suite 420
Boston   MA   02120-2140
Phone 617-236-7210 (Voice and TTY)
   Fax 617-572-2094   800 1-800-331-0688 in MA
E-mail fcsninfo@fcsn.org
Web www.fcsn.org
Serving Statewide

Michigan
CAUSE

Patricia   Keller
6412 Centurion Drive, Suite 130
Lansing   MI   48917
Phone 517-886-9167
   Fax 517-886-9366   800 1-800-221-9105 in MI
E-mail info@causeonline.org
Web www.causeonline.org
Serving Statewide

Montana
Parents Let's Unite for Kids

Dennis   Moore
516 North 32nd Street
Billings   MT   59101
Phone 406-255-0540
   Fax 406-255-0523   800 1-800-222-7585 in MT
E-mail plukinfo@pluk.org
Web www.pluk.org
Serving Statewide

Nevada
Nevada Parents Encouraging Parents (PEP)

Karen   Taycher
2355 Red Rock Street, #106
Las Vegas   NV   89146
Phone 702-388-8899
   Fax 702-388-2966   800 1-800-216-5188
E-mail pepinfo@nvpep.org
Web www.nvpep.org
Serving Statewide

New Hampshire
Parent Information Center

Bonnie   Dunham
P.O. Box 2405
Concord   NH   03302-2405
Phone 603-224-7005 (Voice & TDD)
   Fax 603-224-4365   800 1-800-232-0986 in NH
E-mail hthalheimer@parentinformationcenter.org
Web www.parentinformationcenter.org
Serving Statewide

New Jersey
Statewide Parent Advocacy Network (SPAN)

Debra   Fernandez
35 Halsey Street, 4th Floor
Newark   NJ   07102
Phone 973-642-8100
   Fax 973-642-8080   800 1-800-654-SPAN
E-mail AutinD@aol.com Df77starfish@aol.com
Web www.spannj.org
Serving Statewide

New Mexico
Parents Reaching Out

Larry   Fuller
1920 "B" Columbia Drive SE
Albuquerque   NM   87106
Phone 505-247-0192
   Fax 505-247-1345   800 1-800-524-5176 in NM
E-mail prodreamaker1@aol.com
Web www.parentsreachingout.org
Serving Statewide

New York
Advocates for Children of NY

Ana   Espada
151 West 30th Street, 5th Floor
New York   NY   10001
Phone 212-947-9779
   Fax 212-947-9790   800
E-mail aespada@advocatesforchildren.org
Web www.advocatesforchildren.org
Serving Five boroughs of New York City

Funded Centers, by State

New York
Resources for Children with Special Needs, Inc.

Karen   Schlesinger
116 East 16th Street, 5th Floor
New York NY 10003
Phone 212-677-4650
Fax 212-254-4070   800
E-mail info@resourcesnyc.org
Web www.resourcesnyc.org
Serving New York City (Bronx, Brooklyn, Manhattan, Queens, Staten Island)

Oklahoma
Oklahoma Parents Center, Inc.

Sharon   Bishop
4600 Southeast 29th Street, Suite 115
Del City OK 73115-4224
Phone 405-619-0500
Fax 405-670-0776   800 1-877-553-IDEA (4332)
E-mail okparentctr@aol.com
Web www.okparents.org
Serving Statewide

North Carolina
Exceptional Children's Assistance Center (ECAC) Inc.

Connie Hawkins /   Mary LaCorte
907 Barra Row, Suite 102 & 103
Davidson NC 28036
Phone 704-892-1321
Fax 704-892-5028   800 1-800-962-6817 NC only
E-mail mlacorte@ecacmail.org
Web www.ecac-parentcenter.org/
Serving Statewide

Oregon
Oregon PTI

Janice   Richards
2295 Liberty Street, NE
Salem OR 97303-6755
Phone 503-581-8156 Voice & TDD
Fax 503-391-0429   800 1-888-505-2673 (OR only)
E-mail orpti@open.org
Web www.open.org/~orpti
Serving Statewide

North Dakota
ND Pathfinder PTI

Kathryn   Erickson
Arrowhead Shopping Center
1600 2nd Avenue Southwest, Suite 19
Minot ND 58701-3459
Phone 701-837-7500 voice / 701-837-7501 TDD
Fax 701-837-7548   800 1-800-245-5840
E-mail ndpath01@ndak.net
Web www.pathfinder.minot.com
Serving Statewide

Pennsylvania
Parent Education Network

Louise   Thieme
2107 Industrial Hwy
York PA 17402-2223
Phone 717-600-0100 Voice & TTY
Fax 717-600-8101   800 1-800-522-5827 in PA
E-mail pen@parentednet.org
Web www.parentednet.org
Serving Statewide, 1-800-441-5028 (Spanish in PA)

Ohio
OCECD (PTI)

Margaret   Burley
Bank One Building
165 West Center St., Suite 302
Marion OH 43302-3741
Phone 740-382-5452 Voice & TDD
Fax 740-383-6421   800 1-800-374-2806
E-mail ocecd@gte.net
Web www.ocecd.org
Serving Statewide except SW Region

Puerto Rico
APNI

Carmen   Sellés deVilá
P.O. Box 21280
San Juan PR 00928-1280
Phone 787-763-4665
Fax 787-765-0345   800 1-800-981-8492
E-mail centroinfo@apnipr.org
Web www.apnipr.org
Serving Island of Puerto Rico

Funded Centers, by State

Rhode Island
RI Parent Info Network, Inc. (RIPIN)

Cheryl   Collins
175 Main Street
Pawtucket RI 02860-4101
Phone 401-727-4144
Fax 401-724-0867   800 1-800-464-3399 in RI
E-mail collins@ripin.org
Web www.ripin.org
Serving Statewide

Texas
Partners Resource Network - PATH Project

Alice   Robertson
1090 Longfellow Drive
Beaumont TX 77630
Phone 409-898-4684 Voice & TDD
Fax 409-898-4869   800 1-800-866-4726 in TX
E-mail partnersresource@sbcglobal.net
Web www.PartnersTX.org
Serving Serving Dallas, Fort Worth, Austin, Wichita Falls,
Southeast and East Texas

South Carolina
PRO-PARENTS

Mary   Eaddy
652 Bush River Road, Suite 218
Columbia SC 29210
Phone 803-772-5688
Fax 803-772-5341   800 1-800-759-4776 in SC
E-mail proparents@aol.com
Web www.proparents.org
Serving Statewide

Utah
Utah Parent Center

Helen   Post
2290 East 4500 S., Suite 110
Salt Lake City UT 84117-4428
Phone 801-272-1051
Fax 801-272-8907   800 1-800-468-1160 in UT
E-mail helen@utahparentcenter.org
Web www.utahparentcenter.org
Serving Statewide

South Dakota
South Dakota Parent Connection

Lynn   Boettcher Fjellanger
3701 West 49th Street, Suite 200B
Sioux Falls SD 57106
Phone 605-361-3171 Voice & TDD
Fax 605-361-2928   800 1-800-640-4553 in SD
E-mail lynnbf@sdparent.org
Web www.sdparent.org
Serving Statewide

Vermont
Vermont Parent Information Center

Connie   Curtin
1 Mill Street, Suite 310
Burlington VT 05401
Phone 802-658-5315 Voice & TDD
Fax 802-658-5395   800 1-800-639-7170 in VT
E-mail vpic@vtpic.com
Web www.vtpic.com
Serving Statewide

Tennessee
Support & Training for Exceptional Parents, Inc.

Nancy   Diehl
712 Professional Plaza
Greeneville TN 37745
Phone 423-639-0125 voice / 423-639-8802 TDD
Fax 423-636-8217   800 1-800-280-STEP in TN
E-mail information@tnstep.org
Web www.tnstep.org
Serving Statewide

Virginia
Parent Educational Advocacy Training Center

Cherie   Takemoto
6320 Augusta Drive, Suite 1200
Springfield VA 22150
Phone 703-923-0010
Fax 703-923-0030   800 1-800-869-6782 VA only
E-mail takemoto@peatc.org
Web www.peatc.org
Serving Statewide

Funded Centers, by State

Washington
Washington PAVE

Joanne   Butts
6316 South 12th Street, Suite B
Tacoma   WA   98465-1900
Phone 253-565-2266 (Voice & TDD)
Fax 253-566-8052   800 1-800-572-7368 in WA
E-mail jbutts@washingtonpave.com
Web www.washingtonpave.org
Serving Statewide

Minnesota
PACER Center, Inc.

Paula Goldberg/   Virginia Richardson
8161 Normandale Boulevard
Minneapolis   MN   55437-1044
Phone 952-838-9000 voice 952-838-0190 TTY
Fax 952-838-0199   800 1-800-537-2237 in MN
E-mail pacer@pacer.org
Web www.pacer.org
Serving Statewide

Specialized Training of Military Parents (STOMP)

Heather   Hebdon
6316 South 12th Street, Suite B
Tacoma   WA   98465-1900
Phone 253-565-2266 Voice & TTY
Fax 253-566-8052   800 1-800-5PARENT
E-mail stomp@washingtonpave.com
Web www.stompproject.org
Serving Military Families; U.S. Military installations; and as a
resource for parent centers and others.

California
Exceptional Parents Unlimited

Bobbie   Coulbourne
4440 North First Street
Fresno   CA   93726
Phone 559-229-2000
Fax 559-229-2956   800
E-mail bcoulbourne@exceptionalparents.org
Web www.exceptionalparents.org
Serving Central California

West Virginia
West Virginia Parent Training and Information

Pat   Haberbosch
371 Broaddus Ave
Clarksburg   WV   26301
Phone 304-624-1436 Voice & TTY
Fax 304-624-1438   800 1-800-281-1436 in WV
E-mail wvpti@aol.com
Web www.wvpti.org
Serving Statewide

Virgin Islands
V.I. FIND

Catherine Rehema   Glenn
#2 Nye Gade
PO Box 11670
St. Thomas US   VI   00802
Phone 340-774-1662
Fax 340-774-1662   800
E-mail vifind@islands.vi
Web www.taalliance.org/ptis/vifind/
Serving Virgin Islands

Wyoming
Parent Information Center

Terri   Dawson
5 North Lobban
Buffalo   WY   82834
Phone 307-684-2277 Voice & TDD
Fax 307-684-5314   800 800-660-9742 WY only
E-mail tdawson@wpic.org
Web www.wpic.org
Serving Statewide

Mississippi
Parent Partners

Terry   Burton
5 Old River Place, Suite 101
Jackson   MS   39202
Phone 601-354-3302
Fax 601-354-2426   800 1-800-366-5707 in MS
E-mail tburton@ParentPartners.org
Web www.ParentPartners.org
Serving Statewide

Funded Centers, by State

New York
Sinergia/Metropolitan Parent Center

Donald　　　　Lash
15 West 65th St., 6th Floor
New York　NY　10023
Phone 212-496-1300
　Fax 212-496-5608　　800
E-mail dlash@sinergiany.org
Web www.sinergiany.org
Serving New York City & Long Island

Louisiana　　　*
Pyramid Community Parent Resource Center

D.J. and Ursula　　　Markey
2552 St. Phillip Street
New Orleans　LA　70119
Phone 504-827-0610
　Fax 504-827-2999　　800
E-mail PyramidCPRC@aol.com
Web
Serving Greater New Orleans Metropolitan Area

California　　　*
Loving Your Disabled Child

Theresa　　　　Cooper
4528 Crenshaw Boulevard
Los Angeles　CA　90043-1221
Phone 323-299-2925
　Fax 323-299-4373　　800 1-888-839-2129
E-mail info@lydc.org
Web www.lydc.org
Serving Most of LA County

California
TASK, San Diego

Brenda　　　　Smith
4550 Kearny Villa Road #102
San Diego　CA　92123
Phone 858-874-2386
　Fax 858-874-0123　　800
E-mail taskca@yahoo.com
Web www.taskca.org
Serving City of San Diego and Imperial County

New York　　　*
United We Stand

Lourdes　　　　Rivera-Putz
202 Union Avenue, Suite L
Brooklyn　NY　11211
Phone 718-302-4313
　Fax 718-302-4315　　800
E-mail uwsofny@aol.com
Web www.unitedwestandofny.org
Serving

California　　　*
Parents of Watts

Alice　　　　Harris
10828 Lou Dillon Ave
Los Angeles　CA　90059
Phone 323-566-7556
　Fax 323-569-3982　　800
E-mail egertonf@hotmail.com
Web
Serving With Loving Your Disabled Child

California　　　*
Vietnamese Parents of Disabled Children Assoc., Inc.

Hung　　　　Nguyen
7526 Syracuse Avenue
Stanton　CA　90680
Phone 310-370-6704
　Fax 310-542-0522　　800
E-mail hgnguyen@vpdca.org
Web www.VPDCA.org
Serving LA County and Orange County

Washington　　　*
Parent to Parent Power

Yvone　　　　Link
1118 South 142nd Street, Suite B
Tacoma　WA　98444
Phone 253-531-2022
　Fax 253-538-1126　　800
E-mail yvone_link@yahoo.com
Web www.p2ppower.org
Serving Asian families in Wstrn WA - also Canada border

Funded Centers, by State

California
Support for Families of Children with Disabilities

Juno   Duenas
2601 Mission Street #606
San Francisco CA   94110-3111
Phone 415-282-7494
Fax 415-282-1226   800
E-mail jduenas@supportforfamilies.org
Web www.supportforfamilies.org
Serving San Francisco

California
Exceptional Family Support, Education and Advocacy

Kathleen   Lowrance
6319 A Skyway
Paradise CA   95969
Phone 530-226-5129
Fax 530-226-5141   800 1-888-263-1311
E-mail sklowrance@aol.com
Web www.sea-center.org
Serving

Pennsylvania   *
Mentor Parent Program, Inc.

Gail   Walker
PO Box 47
Pittsfield PA   16340
Phone 814-563-3470
Fax 814-563-3445   800 1-888-447-1431 (in PA)
E-mail gwalker@westpa.net
Web www.mentorparent.org
Serving Rural Northwest Pennsylvania

Arizona
Pilot Parents of Southern Arizona

Lynn   Kallis
2600 North Wyatt Drive
Tucson AZ   85712
Phone 520-324-3150
Fax 520-324-3152   800 1-877-365-7220
E-mail ppsa@pilotparents.org
Web www.pilotparents.org
Serving Southern AZ

Texas
Special Kids, Inc. (SKI)

Agnes A.   Johnson
P.O. Box 266958
Houston TX   77207-6958
Phone 713-734-5355
Fax 713-643-6291   800
E-mail speckids@aol.com
Web Houston Independent School Districts: South, South
Serving Central & Central

New York
The Advocacy Center

Jason   Blackwell
590 South Avenue
Averill Court
Rochester NY   14620
Phone 585-546-1700
Fax 585-546-7069   800 800-650-4967 in NY
E-mail blackwell@advocacycenter.com
Web www.advocacycenter.com
Serving Statewide except NY City

Missouri
Missouri Parents Act (MPACT)

Mary Kay   Savage
One West Armour, Suite 302
Kansas City MO   64111
Phone 816-531-7070 / 816-931-2992 TDD
Fax 816-531-4777   800
E-mail msavage@ptimpact.com
Web www.ptimpact.com
Serving Statewide

Wisconsin
Native American Family Empowerment Center

Don   Rosin
Great Lakes InterTribal Council
2932 Highway 47N, P.O. Box 9
Lac du Flambeau WI   54538
Phone 715-588-3324
Fax 715-588-7900   800 1-800-472-7207
E-mail drosin@glitc.org
Web
Serving

Funded Centers, by State

District of Columbia
Advocates for Justice and Education

Kim   Jones
2041 Martin Luther King Ave., SE, Suite 205
Washington   DC   20020
Phone 202-678-8060
   Fax 202-678-8062   **800** 1-888-327-8060
E-mail kim.jones@aje-DC.org
   Web www.AJE-DC.org
Serving District of Columbia

Virginia   *
PADDA, Inc.

Mark   Jacob
813 Forrest Drive, Suite 3
Newport News   VA   23606
Phone 757-591-9119
   Fax 757-591-8990   **800** 1-888-337-2332
E-mail mjacob@padda.org
   Web www.padda.org
Serving Southeastern VA

Florida   *
Parent to Parent of Miami, Inc.

Isabel   Garcia
7990 SW 117th Ave, Suite 201
Miami   FL   33183
Phone 305-271-9797
   Fax 305-271-6628   **800** 1-800-527-9552
E-mail info@ptopmiami.org
   Web www.ptopmiami.org
Serving Miami, Dade and Monroe Counties

Wisconsin
Wisconsin FACETS (PTI)

Jan Serak   Charlotte Price
2714 North Dr. Martin Luther King Dr.
Milwaukee   WI   53212
Phone 414-374-4645 / 414-374-4635 TTD
   Fax 414-374-4655   **800** 1-877-374-4677
E-mail wifacets@execpc.com
   Web www.wifacets.org
Serving Statewide

Mississippi   *
Project Empower

Agnes   Johnson
136 South Poplar Street
PO Box 1733
Greenville   MS   38702-1733
Phone 662-332-4852
   Fax 662-332-1622   **800** 1-800-337-4852
E-mail empower@tecinfo.com
   Web
Serving Six EMPOWER Counties

Pennsylvania   *
Hispanos Unidos para Ninos Excepcionales
(Hispanics United for Exceptional Children)
Luz   Hernandez
Buena Vista Plaza
166 W. Lehigh Ave., Suite 400
Philadelphia   PA   19133-3838
Phone 215-425-6203
   Fax 215-425-6204   **800**
E-mail huneinc@aol.com
   Web
Serving American Street Empowerment Zone

Texas   *
The Arc of Texas in the Rio Grande Valley
Parents Supporting Parents Network
Leticia   Padilla
601 North Texas Boulevard
Weslaco   TX   78596
Phone 956-447-8408
   Fax 956-973-9503   **800** 1-888-857-8688
E-mail lpadilla@rgv.rr.com
   Web www.thearcoftexas.org
Serving Rio Grande Valley of Southern Texas

Native American Families Together Parent Center

Chris Curry &   Susan Banks
129 West Third
Moscow   ID   83843
Phone 208-885-3500
   Fax 208-885-3628   **800** 1-877-205-7501
E-mail NAFT@moscow.com
   Web www.nativefamilynetwork.com
Serving Nation-wide resource for Native American families, tribes, communities, parent centers, and others.

Funded Centers, by State

South Carolina *
Parent Training & Resource Center

Beverly   McCarty
MUSC-College of Health Professions
19 Hagood Ave, Suite 910, PO Box 250822
Charleston   SC   29425
Phone 843-792-3025
Fax 843-792-1107   800
E-mail mccartyb@musc.edu
Web www.ptrc.org
Serving Tri-county: Charleston, Berkeley, and Dorchester

New Mexico *
EPICS Project

Martha   Gorospe-Charlie
Abrazos Family Support Services
PO Box 788
Bernalillo   NM   87004
Phone 505-867-3396
Fax 505-867-3398   800
E-mail info@abrazosnm.org
Web www.abrazosnm.org
Serving New Mexico 22 American Indian Communities

Kentucky *
FIND of Louisville

Robin   Young Porter
1146 South Third Street
Louisville   KY   40203
Phone 502-584-1239
Fax 502-584-1261   800
E-mail find@councilonmr.org
Web www.findoflouisville.org
Serving Jefferson County

Minnesota *
discapacitados abriendose caminos

Ana   Perez de Perez
608 Smith Avenue South
St. Paul   MN   55107
Phone 651-293-1748
Fax 651-293-1744   800
E-mail discapacitados@comcast.net
Web
Serving

North Carolina *
Hope Parent Resource Center/Burke County Parent
Resource Center
Vickie   Dieter
300 Enola Road
Morganton   NC   28655
Phone 828-438-6540 (Eng/Span) 828-433-2825 (Hmong)
Fax 828-433-2821   800
E-mail vbdieter@charter.net
Web Burke County
Serving

Tennessee *
Nashville Family Alliance Center

holly lu   conant rees
111 North Wilson Boulevard
Nashville   TN   37205
Phone 615-321-5699
Fax 615-322-9184   800
E-mail hlu1030@aol.com
Web www.SPAN-TN.org
Serving

Colorado *
El Grupo Vida's Parent Resource Center

Rhonda   Williams
126 West 5th Avenue
Denver   CO   80204
Phone 303-864-1900
Fax 303-864-0035   800 1-800-284-0251
E-mail elgrupovida@peakparent.org
Web www.peakparent.org
Serving

Nebraska
PTI Nebraska

Glenda   Davis
3135 North 93rd Street
Omaha   NE   68134
Phone 402-346-0525
Fax 402-934-1479   800 1-800-284-8520
E-mail info@pti-nebraska.org
Web www.pti-nebraska.org
Serving Statewide

Funded Centers, by State

Wisconsin *
Wisconsin FACETS (CPRC)

Sue Endress
2714 North Dr. Martin Luther King Dr.
Milwaukee WI 53212
Phone 414-374-4645 / 414-374-4635 TTD
Fax 414-374-4655 800 1-877-374-4677
E-mail wifacets@execpc.com
Web www.wifacets.org
Serving Milwaukee

California *
Sickle Cell Health Network
Oakland PEACE CPRC
Anita Haynes
610 16th Street, Suite 214
Oakland CA 94612
Phone 510-628-0610
Fax 510-628-0611 800
E-mail sicklecellnet@sbcglobal.net
Web
Serving

Virgin Islands *
Country/ Hills Project

Catherine Rehema Glenn
#2 Nye Gade
St. Thomas US VI 00802
Phone 340-774-1662
Fax 340-774-1662 800
E-mail vifind@islands.vi
Web www.taalliance.org/ptis/vifind/
Serving Virgin Islands

Michigan *
Association for Children's Mental Health

Joy Craig
6900 McGraw
Detroit MI 48210
Phone 313-895-2860
Fax 313-895-2867 800
E-mail detroitacmh@sbcglobal.net
Web
Serving

Michigan
Tri-County Partnership

Pat Keller
NW Activity Center
18100 Meyers, Suite 307
Detroit MI 48235
Phone 313-863-0813
Fax 313-863-8048 800 1-800-298-4424
E-mail infodetroit@causeonline.org
Web Wayne, Oakland, Macomb Counties
Serving

Maine *
Southern Maine Parent Awareness

Kimberley Megrath
886 Main Street, Suite 303
Sanford ME 04073
Phone 207-324-2337
Fax 207-324-5621 800 1-800-564-9696 in ME
E-mail kimberley.megrath@somepa.org
Web www.somepa.org
Serving York and Cumberland County and Lewiston

Alaska *
LINKS-MatSu Parent Resource Center

P.O. Box 876007
Wassila AK 99687
Phone 907-373-3632
Fax 907-373-3620 800
E-mail links@gci.net
Web www.linksprc.org
Serving Mat-Su Valley

Illinois
Family Matters (ARC Community Support Systems)

Debbie Einhorn
2502 South Veterans Drive
Effingham IL 62401
Phone 217-347-5428
Fax 217-347-5119 800 1-866-436-7842
E-mail info@fmptic.org or deinhorn@arc-css.org (director)
Web www.fmptic.org
Serving Statewide except Chicago

Funded Centers, by State

Idaho *
Idaho Parents Unlimited, Inc. (CPRC)

Evelyn   Mason
600 North Curtis Road, Suite 100
Boise   ID   83706
Phone 208-342-5884 Voice & TDD
  Fax 208-342-1408   800 1-800-242-4785
E-mail evelyn@ipulidaho.org
  Web www.ipulidaho.org
Serving Statewide

Arkansas
FOCUS, Inc.

Shelby   Knight
2809 Forest Home Road
Jonesboro AR 72401
Phone 870-935-2750
  Fax 870-931-3755   800
E-mail focus_inc2@hotmail.com
  Web www.ArkansasPTI.org
Serving 30 counties in NE Arkansas

Texas *
El Valle CPRC

Cynthia   Caballero
530 South Texas, Suite J
Weslaco   TX   78596
Phone 956-969-3611
  Fax 956-969-8761   800 1-800-680-0255 in TX only
E-mail texasfiestaedu@tiagris.com
  Web www.tfepoder.org/el_valle.html
Serving Starr, Willacy, Cameron & Hidalgo Counties

North Carolina *
F.I.R.S.T.

Janet   Price-Ferrell
PO Box 802
Asheville NC   28802
Phone 828-277-1315
  Fax 828-277-1321   800 1-877-633-3178
E-mail FIRSTwnc@aol.com
  Web Buncombe, Madison, Henderson, Yancey Co.
Serving

Texas
Partners Resource Network - PEN Project

Jon   Howell
1001 Main Street, Suite 804
Lubbock   TX   79401
Phone 806-762-1434
  Fax 806-762-1628   800 1-877-762-1435 in TX
E-mail wtxpen@sbcglobal.net
  Web www.PartnersTX.org
Serving Amarillo, Lubbock, Abilene, San Angelo, and El Paso

Washington *
Rural Outreach

Peggy   Scuderi
805 Southwest Alcora
Pullam WA   99163
Phone 509-595-5440
  Fax   800
E-mail routreach@adelphia.net
  Web
Serving

Ohio
OCECD (PTI-Early Childhood)

Lee Ann   Derugen
Bank One Building
165 West Center St., Suite 302
Marion   OH   43302-3741
Phone 740-382-5452 Voice & TDD
  Fax 740-383-6421   800 1-800-374-2806
E-mail ocecd@gte.net
  Web www.ocecd.org
Serving Southwest Ohio

Iowa *
Family Link CPRC

Carla   Wyatt
Orpheum Building
520 Pierce Street, Suite 360
Sioux City   IA   51101
Phone 712-255-7722
  Fax 712-239-4685   800
E-mail thompsonwyattfam@aol.com
  Web
Serving

Funded Centers, by State

American Samoa   *
CPRC in American Samoa

Elda   Najera-Suisala
PO Box 2191
Pago Pago AS 96799
  Phone 684-699-6621
     Fax   800
  E-mail suisala@blueskynet.as; cfldd@samoatelco.com
    Web http://www.taalliance.org/ptis/amsamoa/
Serving

Texas
Partners Resource Network - TEAM Project

Maria   Hurtado
2547 Blossom Street
San Antonio TX 78217
  Phone 210-832-8945
    Fax 210-832-8959   800 1-877-832-8945
  E-mail partnersteam@sbcglobal.net
    Web www.PartnersTX.org
  Serving San Antonio, Houston, Lower Rio Grande Valley

APPENDIX 14:
DSM-IV CRITERIA FOR ATTENTION DEFICITY/HYPERACTIVITY DISORDER

A. According to the DSM-IV, a person with Attention Deficit/Hyperactivity Disorder must have either (1) or (2):

(1) Six (or more) of the following symptoms of inattention have persisted for at least 6 months to a degree that is maladaptive and inconsistent with developmental level:

INATTENTION

(a) often fails to give close attention to details or makes careless mistakes in school work, work, or other activities

(b) often has difficulty sustaining attention in tasks or play activities

(c) often does not seem to listen when spoken to directly

(d) often does not follow through on instructions and fails to finish schoolwork, chores, or duties in the workplace (not due to oppositional behavior or failure to understand instructions)

(e) often has difficulty organizing tasks and activities

(f) often avoids, dislikes, or is reluctant to engage in tasks that require sustained mental effort (such as schoolwork or homework)

(g) often loses things necessary for tasks or activities (e.g., toys, school assignments, pencils, books, or tools)

(h) is often easily distracted by extraneous stimuli

(i) is often forgetful in daily activities

(2) Six (or more) of the following symptoms of hyperactivity-impulsivity have persisted for at least 6 months to a degree that is maladaptive and inconsistent with developmental level:

HYPERACTIVITY

(a) often fidgets with hands or feet or squirms in seat

(b) often leaves seat in classroom or in other situations in which remaining seated is expected

(c) often runs about or climbs excessively in situations in which it is inappropriate (in adolescents or adults, may be limited to subjective feelings or restlessness)

(d) often has difficulty playing or engaging in leisure activities quietly

(e) is often "on the go" or often acts as if "driven by a motor"

(f) often talks excessively

(g) often blurts out answers before questions have been completed

(h) often has difficulty awaiting turn

(i) often interrupts or intrudes on others (e.g., butts into conversations or games)

B. Some hyperactive-impulsive or inattentive symptoms that caused impairment were present before age 7 years.

C. Some impairment from the symptoms is present in two or more settings (e.g., at school and at home).

D. There must be clear evidence of clinically significant impairment in social, academic, or occupational functioning.

E. The symptoms do not occur exclusively during the course of a Pervasive Developmental Disorder, Schizophrenia, or other Psychotic Disorder and are not better accounted for by another mental disorder (e.g., Mood Disorder, Anxiety Disorder, Disassociative Disorder, or a Personality Disorder).

ATTENTION DEFICIT/HYPERACTIVITY DISORDER, COMBINED TYPE:

If both Criteria A1 and A2 are met for the past 6 months.

ATTENTION DEFICIT/HYPERACTIVITY DISORDER, PREDOMINANTLY INATTENTIVE TYPE:

If Criterion A1 is met but Criterion A2 is not met for the past 6 months.

ATTENTION DEFICIT/HYPERACTIVITY DISORDER, PREDOMINANTLY HYPERACTIVE-IMPULSIVE TYPE:

If Criterion A2 is met but Criterion A1 is not met for the past 6 months.

Source: American Psychiatric Association: Diagnostic and Statistical Manual of Mental Disorders, Fourth Edition.

NUMBER OF CHILDREN AGED 3 TO 21 YEARS OLD IN FEDERALLY SUPPORTED PROGRAMS FOR THE DISABLED, BY TYPE OF DISABILITY (1976/1977-2000/2001) (IN THOUSANDS)

TYPE OF DISABILITY	1976-77	1980-81	1988-89	1989-90	1990-91	1991-92	1992-93	1993-94	1994-95	1995-96	1996-97	1997-98	1998-99	1999-2000	2000-01
All disabilities	3,694	4,144	4,529	4,631	4,761	4,941	5,111	5,309	5,378	5,573	5,729	5,903	6,054	6,190	6,293
Specific learning disabilities	796	1,462	1,984	2,047	2,129	2,232	2,351	2,408	2,489	2,579	2,649	2,725	2,789	2,830	2,842
Speech or language impairments	1,302	1,168	964	971	985	996	994	1,014	1,015	1,022	1,043	1,056	1,068	1,078	1,084
Mental retardation	961	830	560	547	535	537	518	536	555	570	579	589	597	600	599

TYPE OF DISABILITY	1976-77	1980-81	1988-89	1989-90	1990-91	1991-92	1992-93	1993-94	1994-95	1995-96	1996-97	1997-98	1998-99	1999-2000	2000-01
Emotional disturbance	283	347	372	380	390	399	400	414	427	438	445	453	462	468	472
Hearing impairments	88	79	56	57	58	60	60	64	64	67	68	69	70	70	70
Orthopedic impairments	87	58	47	48	49	51	52	56	60	63	66	67	69	71	72
Other health impairments	141	98	50	52	55	58	65	82	106	133	160	190	221	254	292
Visual impairments	38	31	22	22	23	24	23	24	24	25	25	25	26	26	25
Multiple disabilities	n/a	68	83	86	96	97	102	108	88	93	98	106	106	111	121
Deaf-blindness	n/a	3	1	2	1	1	1	1	1	1	1	1	2	2	1
Autism and traumatic brain injury	n/a	n/a	n/a	n/a	n/a	5	19	24	29	39	44	54	67	80	94
Developmental delay	n/a	n/a	n/a	n/a	n/a	n/a	n/a	n/a	n/a	n/a	n/a	4	12	19	28
Preschool disabled	n/a	n/a	391	418	441	482	525	579	519	544	552	564	568	582	592

Source: U.S. Department of Education, Office of Special Education and Rehabilitative Services.

APPENDIX 16:
SAMPLE INDIVIDUALIZED EDUCATION
PROGRAM

Student Name _____

Date of Meeting to Develop or Review IEP_____

Present Levels of Educational Performance _____

_____

_____

Measurable Annual Goals (Including Benchmarks or Short-Term
Objectives) _____

_____

_____

Special Education and Related Services _____

_____

_____

Start Date _____

    Location _____

    Frequency _____

    Duration _____

Supplementary Aids and Services _____

_____

_____

    Start Date _____

    Location _____

    Frequency _____

    Duration _____

Program Modifications or Supports for School Personnel _____

_____

_____

Start Date _____

   Location _____

   Frequency _____

   Duration _____

Explanation of Extent, if Any, to Which Child Will Not Participate with Nondisabled Children _____

_____

_____

Administration of State and District-wide Assessments of Student Achievement

Any Individual Modifications In Administration Needed For Child To Participate In State Or District-wide Assessment(s)_____

_____

_____

If IEP Team Determines That Child Will Not Participate In A Particular State Or District-Wide Assessment

   Why isn't the assessment appropriate for the child? _____

   _____

   How will the child be assessed? _____

   _____

How Child's Progress Toward Annual Goals Will Be Measured

_____

How Child's Parents Will Be Regularly Informed Of Child's Progress Toward Annual Goals And Extent To Which Child's Progress Is Sufficient To Meet Goals By End of Year

_____

_____

(Beginning at age 16 or younger if determined appropriate by IEP team) Statement of Needed Transition Services, Including, If Appropriate, Statement Of Interagency Responsibilities Or Any Needed Linkages

_____

_____

[In a state that transfers rights to the student at the age of majority, the following information must be included beginning at least one year before the student reaches the age of majority]:

The student has been informed of the rights under Part B of IDEA, if any, that will transfer to the student on reaching the age of majority ❑

NOTE: For each student with a disability beginning at age 14 (or younger, if appropriate), a statement of the student's transition service needs must be included under the applicable parts of the IEP. The statement must focus on the courses the student needs to take to reach his or her post-school goals.

Source: U.S. Education Department.

APPENDIX 17:

PERCENTAGE OF DISABLED PERSONS AGED 6-21 YEARS OLD RECEIVING EDUCATION SERVICES, BY AGE GROUP AND EDUCATIONAL ENVIRONMENT (1998-1999)

TYPE OF DISABILITY	ALL ENVIRONMENTS	REGULAR CLASS	RESOURCE ROOM	SEPARATE CLASS	PUBLIC-SEPARATE SCHOOL FACILITY	PRIVATE-SEPARATE SCHOOL FACILITY	PUBLIC RESIDENTIAL FACILITY	PRIVATE RESIDENTIAL FACILITY	HOMEBOUND HOSPITAL PLACEMENT
All persons 6-21 years old	100.0	n/a	47.7	28.6	20.2	1.9	1.1	0.4	0.3
Mental retardation	100.0	13.8	29.2	51.1	4.1	0.9	0.3	0.2	0.4
Speech or language impairments	100.0	88.5	6.6	4.5	0.2	0.1	n/a	n/a	0.1
Visual impairments	100.0	49.6	19.4	16.5	4.7	2.1	6.0	1.1	0.6

TYPE OF DISABILITY	ALL ENVIRONMENTS	REGULAR CLASS	RESOURCE ROOM	SEPARATE CLASS	PUBLIC-SEPARATE SCHOOL FACILITY	PRIVATE-SEPARATE SCHOOL FACILITY	PUBLIC RESIDENTIAL FACILITY	PRIVATE RESIDENTIAL FACILITY	HOMEBOUND HOSPITAL PLACEMENT
Emotional disturbance	100.0	25.5	23.0	33.2	7.5	5.8	1.7	1.9	1.4
Orthopedic impairments	100.0	45.6	20.5	27.3	3.7	0.9	0.1	0.1	1.9
Other health impairments	100.0	44.3	33.2	17.2	0.9	0.7	0.1	0.2	3.4
Specific learning disabilities	100.0	45.1	38.4	15.5	0.3	0.3	0.1	0.1	0.2
Deaf-blindness	100.0	14.1	9.4	34.8	18.9	3.7	14.4	2.9	1.7
Multiple disabilities	100.0	10.5	16.6	44.8	16.2	6.7	1.2	1.6	2.3
Hearing impairments	100.0	39.6	18.7	25.3	4.5	2.6	8.2	0.8	0.2
Autism	100.0	20.3	13.1	51.1	7.8	5.7	0.2	1.2	0.4
Traumatic brain injury	100.0	31.2	26.3	29.8	2.6	6.4	0.2	1.1	2.3
Developmental delay	100.0	41.2	28.8	28.3	1.0	0.2	0.1	n/a	0.4

NOTES:

1. Regular class is outside regular class less than 21 percent of the school day.

2. Resource room is outside regular class more than 21 percent of the school day and less than 60 percent of the school day.

3. Separate class is outside the regular class more than 60 percent of the school day.

Source: U.S. Department of Education, Office of Special Education and Rehabilitative Services.

APPENDIX 18:
SPECIAL EDUCATION INFORMATION RESOURCES

AGENCY	ADDRESS	TELEPHONE	WEBSITE
Office of Special Education Programs	U.S. Department of Education Mary E. Switzer Building 330 C Street SW Washington, DC 20202	(202) 205-5507	www.ed.gov/about/offices/list/osers/osep/
National Information Center for Children and Youth with Disabilities (NICHCY)	P.O. Box 1492 Washington, DC 20013	(800) 695-0285	www.nichcy.org
ERIC Clearinghouse on Disabilities and Gifted Education (ERICEC)	1920 Association Drive Reston, VA 20191-1589	(800) 328-0272	ericec.org
Technical Assistance for Parent Centers—the Alliance	PACER Center 4826 Chicago Avenue South Minneapolis, MN 55417-1098	(888) 248-0822	www.taalliance.org
The Council for Exceptional Children	1920 Association Drive Reston, VA 20191-1589	(888) 232-7733	www.ideapractices.org
Families and Advocates Partnerships for Education (FAPE)	PACER Center, 4826 Chicago Avenue South Minneapolis, MN 55417-1098	(888) 248-0822	www.fape.org
National Association of State Directors of Special Education	1800 Diagonal Road, Suite 320, Alexandria, VA 22314	(703) 519-3800	www.nasdse.org

Source: U.S. Education Department.

GLOSSARY

Achievement levels—Achievement levels define what students should know and be able to do at different levels of performance as follows: (1) Basic level denotes partial mastery of prerequisite knowledge and skills that are fundamental for proficient work at each grade; (2) Proficient level represents solid academic performance for each grade assessed, and competency over challenging subject matter, including subject-matter knowledge, application of such knowledge to real-world situations, and analytical skills appropriate to the subject matter; (3) Advanced level signifies superior performance.

Action at Law—A judicial proceeding whereby one party prosecutes another for a wrong done.

Actual Damages—Actual damages are those damages directly referable to the breach or tortious act, and which can be readily proven to have been sustained, and for which the injured party should be compensated as a matter of right.

Alternative Keyboard—Alternative keyboards may be different from standard keyboards in size, shape, layout, or function. They offer individuals with special needs greater efficiency, control, and comfort.

Alternative Schools—Alternative schools serve students whose needs cannot be met in a regular, special education, or vocational school, e.g., schools for potential dropouts; residential treatment centers for substance abuse; schools for chronic truants; and schools for students with behavioral problems.

Ambulation Aids—Devices that help people walk upright, including canes, crutches, and walkers.

American Civil Liberties Union (ACLU)—A nationwide organization dedicated to the enforcement and preservation of rights and civil liberties guaranteed by the federal and state constitutions.

Americans with Disabilities Act (ADA)—A federal law which prohibits discrimination on the basis of a "qualified" disability as set forth in the statute.

Americans with Disability Act Accessibility Guidelines (ADAAG)—Technical standard for accessible design of new construction or alterations adopted by the Department of Justice for places of public accommodation pursuant to Title III of the ADA.

A Nation at Risk—A report published by the U.S. Department of Education in highlighting deficiencies in knowledge of the nation's students and population as a whole in areas such as literacy, mathematics, geography, and basic science.

Appropriations—Budget authority provided through the congressional appropriation process that permits federal agencies to incur obligations and to make payments.

Architectural Barrier—A physical feature of a public accommodation that limits or prevents disabled persons from obtaining the goods or services offered.

Assistive Technology Device—Any item, piece of equipment, or product system, whether acquired commercially off the shelf, modified, or customized, that is used to increase, maintain, or improve functional capabilities of a child with a disability.

Assistive Technology Service—Any service that directly assists a child with a disability in the selection, acquisition, or use of an assistive technology device.

At-risk—Being "at-risk" means having one or more family background or other risk factors that have been found to predict a high rate of school failure—e.g., retention or dropping out—at some time in the future, including having a mother whose education is less than high school, living in a single-parent family, receiving welfare assistance, and living in a household where the primary language spoken is other than English.

Augmentative Communication System—Any system that increases or improves communication of individuals with receptive or expressive communication impairments. The system can include speech, gestures, sign language, symbols, synthesized speech, dedicated communication devices, microcomputers, and other communication systems.

Braille—A raised dot printed language that is used by persons with visual impairments. Each raised dot configuration represents a letter or word combination.

Braille Embossers and Translators—A Braille embosser transfers computer-generated text into embossed braille output. Translation programs convert text scanned in or generated via standard word processing programs into Braille that can be printed on the embosser.

Burden of Proof—The duty of a party to substantiate an allegation or issue to convince the trier of fact as to the truth of their claim.

Capacity—Capacity is the legal qualification concerning the ability of one to understand the nature and effects of one's acts.

Captioning—A text transcript of the audio portion of multimedia products, such as video and television, that is synchronized to the visual events taking place on screen.

Child Abuse—Any form of cruelty to a child's physical, moral or mental well-being.

Child Protective Agency—A state agency responsible for the investigation of child abuse and neglect reports.

Child Welfare—A generic term which embraces the totality of measures necessary for a child's well being; physical, moral and mental.

Child Aged 3 Through 9—The term "child with a disability" for a child aged 3 through 9 may, at the discretion of the State and the local educational agency, include a child: (i) experiencing developmental delays, as defined by the State and as measured by appropriate diagnostic instruments and procedures, in one or more of the following areas: physical development, cognitive development, communication development, social or emotional development, or adaptive development; and (ii) who, by reason thereof, needs special education and related services.

Child With a Disability—In general, refers to a child: (i) with mental retardation, hearing impairments including deafness, speech or language impairments, visual impairments including blindness, serious emotional disturbance, orthopedic impairments, autism, traumatic brain injury, other health impairments, or specific learning disabilities; and (ii) who, by reason thereof, needs special education and related services.

Circumstantial Evidence—Indirect evidence by which a principal fact may be inferred.

Compensatory Revenue—A type of categorical revenue that targets resources to school districts for instruction and other supplemental services for educationally disadvantaged students.

Constitution—The fundamental principles of law which frame a governmental system.

Constitutional Right—Refers to the individual liberties granted by the constitution of a state or the federal government.

Corporal Punishment—Physical punishment as distinguished from pecuniary punishment or a fine; any kind of punishment of, or inflicted on, the body.

Court—The branch of government responsible for the resolution of disputes arising under the laws of the government.

Damages—In general, damages refers to monetary compensation which the law awards to one who has been injured by the actions of another, such as in the case of tortious conduct or breach of contractual obligations.

Delinquent—An infant of not more than a specified age who has violated criminal laws or has engaged in disobedient, indecent or immoral conduct, and is in need of treatment, rehabilitation, or supervision.

Disability—Under the ADA, an individual is considered disabled if he or she (i) is substantially impaired with respect to a major life activity; (ii) has a record of such an impairment; or (iii) is regarded as having an impairment.

Digitized Speech—Human speech that is recorded onto an integrated circuit chip and which has the ability to be played back.

Display—Assistive technology that raises or lowers dot patterns based on input from an electronic device such as a screen reader or text browser.

Due Process Rights—All rights which are of such fundamental importance as to require compliance with due process standards of fairness and justice.

Duty—The obligation, to which the law will give recognition and effect, to conform to a particular standard of conduct toward another.

Educational Attainment—The highest level of schooling attended and completed.

Educational Service Agency—Refers to (A) a regional public multi-service agency: (i) authorized by State law to develop, manage, and provide services or programs to local educational agencies; and (ii) recognized as an administrative agency for purposes of the provision of special education and related services provided within public elementary and secondary schools of the State; and (B) includes any other public institution or agency having administrative control and direction over a public elementary or secondary school.

Electronic Pointing Devices—Electronic pointing devices allow the user to control the cursor on the screen using ultrasound, an infrared beam, eye movements, nerve signals, or brains waves. When used with an on-screen keyboard, electronic pointing devices also allow the user to enter text or data.

Elementary School—A nonprofit institutional day or residential school that provides elementary education, as determined under state law.

English as a Second Language (ESL)—Programs that provide intensive instruction in English for students with limited English proficiency.

Enrollment—The total number of students registered in a given school unit at a given time, generally in the fall of a year.

Environmental Control Unit (ECU)—A system that enables individuals to control various electronic devices in their environment through a variety of alternative access methods, such as switch or voice access. Target devices include lights, televisions, telephones, music players, door openers, security systems, and kitchen appliances. Also referred to as Electronic Aid to Daily Living (EADL).

Equipment—The term "equipment" includes (A) machinery, utilities, and built-in equipment and any necessary enclosures or structures to house such machinery, utilities, or equipment; and (B) all other items necessary for the functioning of a particular facility as a facility for the provision of educational services, including items such as instructional equipment and necessary furniture; printed, published, and audio-visual instructional materials; telecommunications, sensory, and other technological aids and devices; and books, periodicals, documents, and other related materials.

Excess Costs—Those costs that are in excess of the average annual per-student expenditure in a local educational agency during the preceding school year for an elementary or secondary school student, as may be appropriate, and which shall be computed after deducting (A) amounts received: (i) under part B of this title; (ii) under part A of title I of the Elementary and Secondary Education Act of 1965; or (iii) under part A of title VII of that Act; and (B) any State or local funds expended for programs that would qualify for assistance under any of those parts.

Free Appropriate Public Education—Refers to special education and related services that (A) have been provided at public expense, under public supervision and direction, and without charge; (B) meet the standards of the State educational agency; (C) include an appropriate preschool, elementary, or secondary school education in the State involved; and (D) are provided in conformity with the individualized education program required under section 1414(d).

Guardian—A person who is entrusted with the management of the property and/or person of another who is incapable, due to age or incapacity, to administer their own affairs.

Hearing Impairment—An impairment in hearing, whether permanent or fluctuating, that adversely affects a child's educational performance, in the most severe case, because the child is impaired in processing linguistic information through hearing.

High school—A secondary school offering the final years of high school work necessary for graduation.

Indian—An individual who is a member of an Indian tribe.

Indian Tribe—Any Federal or State Indian tribe, band, rancheria, pueblo, colony, or community, including any Alaskan Native village or regional village corporation (as defined in or established under the Alaska Native Claims Settlement Act).

Individualized Education Program (IEP)—A written statement for each child with a disability that is developed, reviewed, and revised in accordance with section 1414(d).

Individuals with Disabilities Education Act (IDEA)—A statute requiring public schools to provide a free public education to disabled children in the least restrictive environment appropriate for the child's needs.

In Loco Parentis—Latin for "in the place of a parent." Refers to an individual who assumes parental obligations and status without a formal, legal adoption.

Infancy—The period prior to reaching the legal age of majority.

Judge—The individual who presides over a court, and whose function it is to determine controversies.

Keyguards—Keyguards are hard plastic covers with holes for each key. Using a keyguard, someone with an unsteady finger or with a pointing device can avoid striking unwanted keys.

Local Educational Agency—A public board of education or other public authority legally constituted within a State for either administrative control or direction of, or to perform a service function for, public elementary or secondary schools in a city, county, township, school district, or other political subdivision of a State, or for such combination of school districts or counties as are recognized in a State as an administrative agency for its public elementary or secondary schools.

Minor—A person who has not yet reached the age of majority.

Modal Grade—The modal grade is the year of school in which the largest proportion of students of a given age are enrolled and classified according to their relative progress in school, i.e., whether the grade or year in which they were enrolled was below, at, or above the modal or typical grade for persons of their age at the time of the survey.

Multiple disabilities—Concomitant impairments—e.g., mental retardation-blindness, mental retardation-orthopedic impairment, etc.—the combination of which causes such severe educational problems that they cannot be accommodated in special education programs solely for one of the impairments. The term does not include deaf-blindness.

Native Language—With reference to an individual of limited English proficiency, means the language normally used by the individual, or in the case of a child, the language normally used by the parents of the child.

Nonprofit—With reference to a school, agency, organization, or institution, means a school, agency, organization, or institution owned and operated by one or more nonprofit corporations or associations no part of the net earnings of which inures, or may lawfully inure, to the benefit of any private shareholder or individual.

Occupational Education—Refers to vocational education programs that prepare students for a specific occupation or cluster of occupations, including agriculture, business, marketing, health care, protective services, trade and industrial, technology, food service, child care, and personal and other services programs.

Onscreen Keyboard—On-screen keyboards are software images of a standard or modified keyboard placed on the computer screen by software. The keys are selected by a mouse, touch screen, trackball, joystick, switch, or electronic pointing device.

Optical Character Recognition and Scanners—Optical character recognition (OCR) software works with a scanner to convert images from a printed page into a standard computer file. A scanner is a device that converts an image from a printed page to a computer file. With optical character recognition software, the resulting computer file can be edited.

Orthopedic Impairments—Refers to a severe orthopedic impairment that adversely affects a child's educational performance, including impairments caused by congenital anomaly, e.g., clubfoot, absence of some member, etc.; impairments caused by disease, e.g., poliomyelitis, bone tuberculosis, etc.; and impairments from other causes, e.g., cerebral palsy, amputations, and fractures or burns that cause contractures.

Other Support Services Staff—Refers to all staff not reported in other categories, including media personnel, social workers, data processors, health maintenance workers, bus drivers, security, cafeteria workers, and other staff.

Outlying Areas—Includes the United States Virgin Islands, Guam, American Samoa, and the Commonwealth of the Northern Mariana Islands.

Parens Patriae—Latin for "parent of his country." Refers to the role of the state as guardian of legally disabled individuals.

Parent—The term "parent" (A) includes a legal guardian; and (B) except as used in sections 1415(b)(2) and 1439(a)(5), includes an individual assigned under either of those sections to be a surrogate parent.

Prima Facie Case—A case which is sufficient on its face, being supported by at least the requisite minimum of evidence, and being free from palpable defects.

Reading literacy—Reading literacy is defined as understanding, using, and reflecting on written texts in order to achieve one's goals, to develop one's knowledge and potential, and to participate in society.

Regular School Districts—A regular school district can be either: (1) a school district that is not a component of a supervisory union; or (2) a school district component of a supervisory union that shares a superintendent and administrative services with other local school districts.

Regular schools—Schools that are part of state and local school systems as well as private elementary/secondary schools, both religiously affiliated and nonsectarian, that are not alternative schools, vocational education schools, special education schools, subcollegiate departments of postsecondary institutions, residential schools for exceptional children, federal schools for American Indians or Alaska Natives, or federal schools on military posts and other federal installations.

Rehabilitation Act of 1973—A disability discrimination statute which preceded and served as a model for the ADA.

Related Services—Refers to transportation, and such developmental, corrective, and other supportive services, including speech-language pathology and audiology services, psychological services, physical and occupational therapy, recreation, including therapeutic recreation, social work services, counseling services, including rehabilitation counseling, orientation and mobility services, and medical services, except that such medical services shall be for diagnostic and evaluation purposes only as may be required to assist a child with a disability to benefit from special education, and includes the early identification and assessment of disabling conditions in children.

Remedial Education—Instruction for a student lacking the reading, writing, mathematics, or other skills necessary to perform college-level work at the level required by the attended institution.

Scale score—Uses a set scale to assess overall achievement in a domain, such as mathematics.

School District—Also referred to as a local education agency (LEA), refers to an education agency at the local level that exists primarily to operate public schools or to contract for public school services.

Screen Enlargement Programs—Screen enlargement programs magnify a portion of the screen, increasing the visibility for some users with limited vision. Most have variable magnification levels. Some screen enlargement programs offer text-to-speech.

Screen Reader—A screen reader is a software program that uses synthesized speech to "speak" graphics and text out loud. This type of program is used by people with limited vision or blindness.

Seating and Positioning Aids—Modifications to wheelchairs or other seating systems that provide greater body stability, upright posture or reduction of pressure on the skin surface.

Secondary School—A nonprofit institutional day or residential school that provides secondary education, as determined under State law, except that it does not include any education beyond grade 12.

Secretary—The term `"Secretary" as used herein refers to the Secretary of Education.

Service Animal—Refers to an animal, such as a guide dog, which has been trained to provide assistance to disabled individuals.

Special education schools—Special education schools provide educational services to students with special physical or mental needs—i.e., students with mental disabilities (such as mental retardation or autism); physical disabilities (such as hearing impairments); or learning disabilities (such as dyslexia).

Specific learning disabilities—A disorder in one or more of the basic psychological processes involved in understanding or in using language, spoken or written, that may manifest itself in an imperfect ability to listen, think, speak, read, write, spell, or do mathematical calculations, including such conditions as perceptual disabilities, brain injury, minimal brain dysfunction, dyslexia, and developmental aphasia. The term does not apply to children who have learning problems that are primarily the result of visual, hearing, or motor disabilities; of mental retardation; of emotional disturbance; or of environmental, cultural, or economic disadvantage.

Speech or language impairments—A communication disorder such as stuttering, impaired articulation, a language impairment, or a voice impairment that adversely affects a child's educational performance.

Standing—The legal right of an individual or group to use the courts to resolve an existing controversy.

State—Refers to each of the 50 States, the District of Columbia, the Commonwealth of Puerto Rico, and each of the outlying areas.

State Educational Agency—The State board of education or other agency or officer primarily responsible for the State supervision of public elementary and secondary schools, or, if there is no such officer or agency, an officer or agency designated by the Governor or by State law.

Status Offender—A child who commits an act which is not criminal in nature, but which nevertheless requires some sort of intervention and disciplinary attention merely because of the age of the offender.

Statute of Limitations—Any law which fixes the time within which parties must take judicial action to enforce rights or thereafter be barred from enforcing them.

Supplementary Aids and Services—Refers to aids, services, and other supports that are provided in regular education classes or other education-related settings to enable children with disabilities to be educated with nondisabled children to the maximum extent appropriate under the applicable statute.

Supreme Court—In most jurisdictions, the Supreme Court is the highest appellate court, including the federal court system.

Talking Word Processors—A talking word processor is a software program that uses synthesized speech to provide auditory feedback of what has been typed.

TTD or TTY—A Telecommunication Device for the Deaf (TTY or TDD) is a device with a keyboard that sends and receives typed messages over a telephone line.

Telecommunications Device for the Deaf (TDD)—An auxiliary aid consisting of a keyboard and display which is attached to a telephone and used by individuals with hearing or speech impairments to communicate on the telephone.

Telecommunications Relay Services (TRS)—A service which enables hearing or speech impaired callers to communicate with each other through a third party communications assistant using a TDD.

Traditional Public School—All public schools that are not public charter schools or Bureau of Indian Affairs-funded schools operated by local public school districts, including regular, special education, vocational/technical, and alternative schools.

Transition Services—Refers to a coordinated set of activities for a student with a disability that (A) are designed within an outcome-oriented process, which promotes movement from school to post-school activities, including post-secondary education, vocational training, integrated employment, including supported employment, continuing and adult education, adult services, independent living, or community participation; (B) are based upon the individual student's needs, taking into account the student's preferences and interests; and (C) include instruction, related services, community experiences, the development of employment and other post-school adult living objectives, and, when appropriate, acquisition of daily living skills and functional vocational evaluation.

Truancy—Willful and unjustified failure to attend school by one who is required to attend.

Unconstitutional—Refers to a statute which conflicts with the United States Constitution rendering it void.

Vocational Education Schools—Vocational schools primarily serve students who are being trained for semi-skilled or technical occupations.

Voice Recognition—Voice recognition allows the user to speak to the computer instead of using a keyboard or mouse to input data or control computer functions.

BIBLIOGRAPHY AND ADDITIONAL RESOURCES

The ACLU Department of Public Education (Date Visited: June 2004) <http:www.aclu.org>

Black's Law Dictionary, Fifth Edition. St. Paul, MN: West Publishing Company, 1979

Edlaw, Inc. (Date Visited: June 2004) <http://www.edlaw.net> June 2004) <http://www.lrp.com>.

The Library of Education (Date Visited: June 2004) <Library@inet.ed.gov>

The United States Department of Education (Date Visited: June 2004) <http://www.ed.gov>

The United States Department of Education Educational Resources Information Center (Date Visited: June 2004) <askeric@ericir.syr.edu>

The United States Department of Education Office of Special Education and Rehabilitative Services (Date Visited: June 2004) <www.ed.gov/offices/osers>